7 ft Heart

By Shawn Mobilio

Dedicated to:

Josh Ruccio and my family

The buzzer sounded to indicate the end of the game, and my knees hit the polished,

wood court. After a hard-fought series, we lost the championship. I looked into my

coach's face, tears rolling down his cheek, and I cried. This was the first time I had not

achieved my goal. It engendered a deep sense of anguish within me, especially

because it involved basketball. Everything Team Image worked for vanished

before our eyes, and there was no way to fix it. I told myself in that moment,

"Work harder so you never feel this pain again."

PART 1

MIDDLE SCHOOL

Chapter 1

The Love of the Game

"Wake up! Wake up, Shawn and Mikey! We have work to do. We need to go practice at Western School."

My brother, Joe, was the captain of our youth basketball team, Team Image. He could be relentless when it came time for practicing, even on weekends. It wasn't easy growing up with divorced parents, and it meant that our father was not home every night. Even though my mom was great, we needed that tough love from our father. This family dynamic sculpted the relationship between the Mobilio brothers. Joe was the oldest and looked after all of us. I, in turn, looked after our youngest brother, Mike. The three amigos! As one would imagine, we were extremely rambunctious and full of energy kids. We were close as brothers, especially because the three of us shared a bedroom in both our mom's house and our dad's house: Mike and I had a bunk bed, while Joe had his own bed.

It was the day after losing the championship, yet we woke up at 6:00 a.m. to head over to the court. Our neighborhood friend, Burim, joined us to play a little two-on-two. We often met up with him and played for hours. Western School was quiet that early in the morning. That is, until we walked on the court. Our warm-up was inspired by a game seven pregame routine for the

NBA finals. I imagined the bleachers filled with screaming fans, invigorated by the thumping music, cheering for us. I believed that if you didn't dream something, you wouldn't achieve it.

The games were intense with no referees or fouls—just four young men battling to see which pair had the stronger will. It was pure heart. We left it out on the court every day. Of course, the losers had a price to pay. The losing pair had to do things for the winners, such as make the drinks or sandwiches, while the four of us watched NBA games. We treated Burim like a fourth brother, and we loved each other. Sure, Joe and Mike would bicker after Burim and I beat them. This didn't change things. It felt great. And I loved winning.

We were new to town. Our mother moved us from Bridgeport, Connecticut, to Naugatuck, Connecticut. When we moved, it put us closer to my mother's sister and their mother. That side of the family is Portuguese. Our mother made sure we went to church, Sunday school, and catechism. We all celebrated our first communion and were confirmed. Religion was an important aspect of our upbringing, and it was largely due to my mother and grandmother.

Our new Catholic church was right next door to the YMCA, and Mom signed us up for basketball leagues. There was a coach who really wanted us to play for his team. He called the house often, trying to find out more about us. On the first day of tryouts, he told the three of us, "I'm going to pick you guys for my team." We looked at him like he was crazy. The draft happened that night, and he once again called our house. He had drafted all three of us. Burim was also drafted but onto a different team. Our new coach, Josh, told us to show up the next morning at Andrew Avenue School for the first practice with our new team, Team Image.

We were a little nervous but excited when we arrived. In Bridgeport, we played pickup games at the Boys and Girls Club. They didn't offer training and the opportunity to be on a team. When we met our new teammates, it was quickly apparent that my brothers and I had the most energy on the squad. Practice was an amazing experience. Coach Josh embodied what we all had—passion, heart, and a love for the game. He wasn't there just to say he was a coach. He was there to teach us how to win.

When practice ended, we were soaked with sweat. I walked past another coach who was coming into the building, smiling. He seemed laid back and confident. He was the coach of a team called Rotary. We had heard there was a player on the team who was about six feet tall and played point guard. It seemed unreal that a middle school kid was that tall! I asked Coach Josh if we were going to play that team, and he said yes. That night, my brothers and I discussed the situation. How were we going to beat that team? We decided it would take hard work. Joe stepped into the role of captain of our team, and he made sure during every practice that we stayed focused on our goal to win the league championship. We needed to practice to win, and we needed to believe we would win.

Chapter 2

Team Image

Team Rotary was our first opponent of the season. It was an early Saturday morning, and we were pumped and ready to go. The point guard for our opponent, the six-foot-tall kid named John, was already in the gym, practicing with his father. After introducing ourselves, we discovered we all went to the same middle school, and John was in eighth grade with Joe. Father and son continued to drill as we waited for our team to arrive. Coach Josh brought us into the locker room for a pregame pep talk. He told us we had worked hard—it was time to show this league who we were. Over the past few years, Coach Josh never had a team who could beat the undefeated Team Rotary. Their winning record included back-to-back championships the previous two years. That speech was the motivation our team needed. My brothers and I felt as though this was our opportunity to show the league how good we were.

The league mandated that there be an A squad and a B squad. Joe and I were on the A squad. Joe was named captain. I realized I was the only sixth grader on this squad and noticeably the smallest. Mikey was put on the B squad, where he was a powerhouse. Without Mikey, Team Image would have been incomplete.

The game started getting physical right at tip-off. John was a one-man show and Rotary's only strong player. His height made him difficult to defend, and it seemed as though the referees favored him. He was good, and he knew it. We also knew it. As the game progressed, Joe was able to come up big with a couple of jump shots to put our team within ten points.

During the second quarter, Coach Josh put the B squad into the game, and it was Mikey's chance to put us in the lead. Seizing the opportunity, he knocked in a few jumpers that put us two points away. The crowd seemed shocked and confused. I could hear whispers saying, "What's going on?" and "Team Rotary usually wins games by enormous margins."

The final quarter buzzer sounded, and the starters played the majority of the minutes. Although I was on the court, I felt as though I wasn't the strongest player. I needed to find my niche in order to succeed. My strategy was to go to the corner, wait for someone to drive, and sink my shot when the ball was passed to me. Shooting was my best skill but when I missed, my teammates often voiced their displeasure with me. Joe could be particularly harsh. Because I was the youngest and smallest on the A squad, I decided to suck it up when they reprimanded me. The members of my squad would punish me by not passing me the ball. While they all dribbled, passed, and shot, I was left to do the best I could out there. The situation stirred up some jealous feelings toward my teammates. I chose to bury those feelings as if their comments didn't bother me, because I wanted my team to win. At my core, I knew the team's success was more important than my personal feelings.

As the clock counted down, Rotary increased their lead to eight points. Joe answered by coming down the lane and performing his famous "spin move" to a jump shot off the glass. It went right in! Team Rotary took a time-out. Joe's move pumped up our whole bench, including Coach Josh. The team was now ready to finish the last five minutes of the game. I looked over to the opponent's bench, and John and his father were grinning at us. Their confident smiles seemed like a bad omen for our team. Just like that, John took over and scored fifteen points in four minutes. Team Image lost the game by twenty points.

We walked to the locker room with our heads down. It was quiet as we sat, drained by this defeat. Coach Josh entered and told us to keep our heads up because we played a hell of game. "We lost by twenty, Coach," I thought to myself. "You never gave up, and we need to get back to working hard," he articulated. He also speculated that we would see Team Rotary again in the championship. Coach Josh was not going to give up on us. His praise made us feel good about our progress. He was also teaching us how to lose and come back from it. We truly loved him.

We went on to win the next five games. Team Image was on fire, and the town knew it. The local paper reported our wins, dubbing our team "The Mobilio Brothers." We were making a name for ourselves. This was a great feeling. On the other hand, there was one team we wanted badly, and it was Team Rotary. They were our next competitors on the regular season game schedule. It would be our second matchup against Team Rotary. This time, we felt we were ready with a great game plan, and we were sticking to it. We would double-team the ball every time John had it.

After the first quarter, we were down by eleven. This didn't look good. Coach was riled up this game, the refs' calls were in favor of the other team, and shots were not falling for us. The B squad came in, and they struggled too. Turnover after turnover, it was pretty embarrassing. We even took a shot on our own basket. Going into the fourth quarter, we were down thirty-five points. We needed some energy. The first possession I got, the left corner was wide open, and I knocked it down. Three points for Shawn! When we needed a spark, I tried to come alive—like the Energizer Bunny. However, Rotary was too much to handle. John was on fire, and his teammates were knocking in shots as well. No one could contain them. As the final buzzer sounded, the scoreboard showed that Rotary had beaten us 60-23. We walked into the locker room, and Coach Josh flipped out. I could tell he was emotionally drained by the way he screamed at us. His level of anger shocked us. It was one thing to lose, but we had been decimated. And Rotary enjoyed it.

Our record at the end of the season was 15-4, a great record, and the best season Coach Josh had in the last few years. When the playoffs began, we were the three seed.

The bracket indicated for us to play the two seed. Rotary, the one seed, would play the four seed. The two winners would then advance to the championship game. After getting the schedule, the three of us sat in our room. This was our chance, and we had this. Listening to Eminem CDs provided good mental motivation to get ready. Practicing drills and shots in the park every night after completing homework gave us the extra practice we needed. The Mobilio brothers had the discipline and desire at a young age to make sacrifices, to do what it would take to be ready. We really wanted to win the whole thing.

It was a Friday night. Fully focused, we walked into the gym at 6:00 p.m. Coach Josh took one look at us, and he knew we were ready. The team needed one win to be in the championship. This was our goal, and we planned to achieve it. During the pregame pep talk, it felt as if God had brought this coach to us for a reason. He was the right coach at the right time. Team Image would have been a different team had someone else coached us.

We dominated the game from the first whistle. The Mobilio brothers were on a mission to give Coach Josh what he had been seeking—a championship. The three of us led the team in drive and heart, and our team was better because of it. When that final buzzer echoed, Team Image was on top and heading to the championship. Coach had tears of joy in his eyes as he spoke to us in the locker room. "I am so proud of our team tonight," he declared. All of our hard work paid off.

Chapter 3

Tight-knit Family and Neighborhood

Alone, I walked to the basketball court up the street to practice shooting. Dribbling with alternating hands, I kept my head up. Sometimes the ball would hit a crack in the cement and bounce off into the street. Looking both ways first, I would run after it. It reminded me of chasing a loose ball during a game. The thrill of not knowing whether a car would drive by felt similar to not knowing if another player would reach the ball first. Once I arrived at the court, I worked on swiveling my head, just as a good point guard should. The championship game was coming up, and I saw myself walking onto the floor. This was my time to prove I belonged on the A squad.

Coach Josh lived right behind the practice court. It would only be a matter of time before he saw me shooting around. I wanted him to see me and know I was ready for the game. My solo practice started with form shooting drills and then free throws. Before leaving to go back home, it was imperative that I sank five free throws in a row. This was particularly important because free throws are often difficult to make at the end of a close game, when the pressure is on, and your legs begin to get tired. There is also a mental challenge involved that has to do with the fact that no one is guarding you. Free throws are high-pressure shots but like most winners, I thrive under pressure. On this particular day, I decided to take a sixth free throw. The shot hit the front rim and bounced out, and I heard a car horn beep. It was Coach Josh. I ran over to him with excitement, shouting, "I just made five in a row, Coach!"

He looked at me and replied, "Good. Now make twenty in a row before you leave the court."

I walked back to the free throw line and thought, "This is going to be difficult." Digging deep, I convinced myself that this is what I had to do to prove my value as a player. On the first attempt, I made seven in a row and missed the eighth. I grunted loudly as I slammed the ball down with frustration. "Keep your elbow tucked in, put backspin on the ball, and follow through!" I instructed myself. As other kids walked by with their parents, it must have been a curious scene to observe a young sixth grader talking out loud to himself while shooting free throws. During my next attempt, I made ten in a row and missed the eleventh. I was quickly growing impatient. Giving up was not part of my nature, so I kept shooting despite the increasing mental fatigue. The biggest game of our lives was coming up. I needed to prevail. "I can do this!"

Without realizing it, the sun was setting, and my watch read 7:00 p.m. I had been out there for three hours. Coach returned home and yelled, "Twenty yet? Not yet? Keep going, Shawn." On the next try, I missed the sixteenth shot. "I'm not going to get mad," I told myself. But I lost it anyway. I was overcome with frustration and chucked the ball into the fence. By this time, I could barely see the rim because it was pitch dark out. I continued to shoot even though I knew my mom would be worried. A set of headlights blinded me, and I recognized the sound of the car horn. It was too late; she was out looking for me. "Shawn, are you crazy? Get in the car!"

"Mom, I can't. I need to make twenty free throws in a row," I replied.

"How? I can't even see a thing."

"Mom, I can see. You just have bad eyes."

She laughed and said, "Get in the car."

"I am at eighteen. Two more, then I will go home," I said. She waited patiently as I took my nineteenth shot. I prayed for it to go in because I knew she was ready to get the belt and chase me around the park. The nineteenth shot went up, swish, all net. "Yes!" I said to myself. "Mom, one more, and we are going home," I called over to her.

"I hope you have food because you're not eating tonight," she stated.

"After this next shot, I'm eating success!" I answered. Sweat was dripping off of me, dehydration was kicking in, and my calves were cramping up. I could barely hold the ball. It felt like twenty pounds, but I was determined to make this shot. I bent my legs, squared to the hoop with my elbow tucked in, and released the ball with great backspin. As I let it go and followed through, my mom yelled, "Come on!" It hit the front of the rim, bounced to the left side, then it rolled to the right side, and finally fell through the net. I had to scream, "Yeah, baby!"

When I got in the car, my mom looked at me and said, "You're going to be very special, Shawn. I believe in your dreams, honey. I love you either way."

I grinned at her and said, "When I make it to the NBA, I will take care of us. You won't have to work again, Mom." She smiled as we drove home.

My brothers gave me grief about where I had been. Mikey was particularly upset with me that I didn't include him. "I needed to do this on my own," I tried to explain to them. The court was my happy place—it was just basketball and me. All my life anxieties would vanish.

Of course, my mom had a plate of food waiting for me that night. My grandmother taught my mother how to cook, and she taught her well. I considered my grandmother as our angel. She was a very old-school Portuguese woman. As a widow, she stayed home most of the time. Every time I walked into her house, she would have a church program on television while she sat and knitted. She often prayed all day long. On my visits to her, she would encourage me to pray to God for any help I needed. "Always keep God first. Keep God in your heart," she would tell us. Vovó, as we called her, made me feel loved by feeding me. If one of us was sick and needed to stay home from school, Vovó would care for us. I would sometimes fake being sick just to hang out with her, eat her food, and have her spoil me. She was the best.

I didn't have all the life complications that my parents had. My mom worked multiple jobs in the cosmetics industry and volunteered, and my dad owned a heating and cooling business. Mom was physically there for us because we lived with her during the week. Despite the long hours my father worked, he always made time for us when we called, and we called a lot. He was a great Italian father who loved the three of us tremendously. My father grew up in a tough part of Bridgeport with his twin brothers and sister. They lost their parents at a young age to cancer. The siblings had to survive on their own with no help. For that reason, I looked up to my paternal uncles and aunt. They are mentally very strong people. Eventually, they started their own family company together. Neither of my parents remarried.

The school bell rang. It made a strange, loud noise that definitely woke you up if you were tired. As I walked into homeroom, everyone was talking about the upcoming big game Friday night. I never paid too much attention to this kind of chatter because most people were saying we had no chance. I chose to ignore the trash talk. However, being the underdogs really fueled our fire as a team. I kind of liked being thought of as an underdog. John walked by me in the hallway and asked me if I was ready. I said, "Yup, see you Friday!" Joe also walked by me, and I could see in his eyes that he was ready to go. He wore these big glasses and sported this little mustache, the Italian and Portuguese in us. It was his eyes that revealed his passion for the game.

As the day ended, I saw Mike walking down the hallway. We sometimes called him "Meatball" because he was small and chubby. He would get mad when we called him that, but he hadn't grown yet. I could tell that he was ready; he always loved shooting the ball.

All three of us met downstairs near the gym at Hillside Middle School at the end of the day. We were tight like special forces—we had each other's backs, especially because we were attending a new school. The three-mile walk home was always a visual journey. Our school was located on a bumpy, cobblestone street. When Mom drove on it, I always felt like I was on the beginning of a roller coaster ride. In certain areas of town, we saw smokers, drugs users, alcoholics, and hoodlums. Joe told us to just keep walking, so we never really paid attention. He would tell us, "You don't need that stuff." Most of these hoodlums wanted to stand out and be cool, but what we saw growing up in Bridgeport was nothing compared to this. One of the reasons our mother moved us to Naugatuck was to get away from the violence and crime. But we learned if you looked for trouble, you would easily be able to find it anywhere.

Burim and another neighborhood friend, Alex, were usually waiting for us on the porch when we arrived home. We all went to the same school, but they got home earlier than we did. Alex also played basketball. We all headed over to the court to run some drills. We had two days before the game, and the town was talking about it. It's a small town, but it felt like we were in the NBA finals.

Chapter 4

The Championship

On Friday night, we made sure our mother took us to the game early. Being early and ready to go was important to us. Mom was pumped to go and be our greatest cheerleader. Mikey and I sat in the back of the car, and Joe was up front with Mom. The atmosphere between the four of us was unnerving, like something big was about to happen. There was no music playing and no talking. Just three boys ready to play some basketball and their mom driving them.

I noticed the gym was packed as we warmed up before the game. I counted about two hundred fans in the stands. This was the biggest game we had played yet. Coach Josh was all smiles as we walked into the locker room to go over the game plan. He said, "Look, we made it here! Now go out and show them who we are!"

The first quarter started, and both teams traded baskets. If there was a loose ball, I was on the floor going for it. We were playing well and kept the score to within five points by the end of the quarter. The second quarter opened with a three-pointer by Rotary and then a layup by Team Image. Both teams were showing they belonged here. The crowd's energy seemed to shift more in favor of Team Image. At the beginning of the third quarter, I sank a corner jump. Joe went to the hoop and earned an old-fashioned three points. This happened when a player went to shoot a basket and was fouled, then get the foul shot; the player can earn three points. We were fighting to keep this game close, but we still had work to do. Before the last quarter started, coach brought us together. The gym felt extremely hot from the combined body temperatures, and we were all sweat-soaked. "We need to get some stops here. Keep it up! You're doing great!" The score was

39-30 in favor of Team Rotary. There was still time to make our move. Everyone on the team powered through.

With two minutes left, Rotary had the ball and was now up by six. They moved it around and executed a play that resulted in a jump shot that splashed through the net. They led by eight, and the clock was ticking. Fortunately, we came down and scored a quick layup, keeping us alive. With one minute left, we were still down by six. Rotary stalled the game, and we were forced to foul. The first shot missed, but the second hit its mark. It wasn't looking good for Team Image. I had the chance for an open three-pointer in the corner and hit the shot, cutting their lead to four. After a Rotary basket, I brought the ball in the corner again. I saw Burim in the bleachers. He stood up, as if he knew I was going to make it. But I didn't. In fact, I didn't even hit the rim. Rotary capitalized on the rebound and with twenty seconds left, we sent them to the line again. Both free throws put them up by nine. Coach Josh took a time-out. I was devastated that I had blown that shot. Coach looked over at me and said, "Keep your head up." We were barely back on the court when the clock ran out. Rotary won the first game of the series, 59-50.

We went into the locker room, and Joe yelled at me. "Dude, you didn't even hit the rim!" The looks on my teammates' faces told me they felt the same way. I had no words. As I sat in the car to go home, I stared out the window, holding in my tears. I didn't want my brothers to see me upset. I kept telling myself not to lose it because I'd make the next one.

That night, I silently cried in bed. It hurt. I wanted to make that shot badly, and I felt I lost that game for us.

After a long weekend, we went off to school with packed lunches. My mom made us a lunch some days, and on other days we would have hot lunch at school. I loved eating chicken patties with fries at school. The best part was mixing ketchup and mayo as my special sauce. In my first period class, my classmates came up to me and sarcastically said, "Nice game Friday night." I wanted so badly to physically react, but I held it together. I realized at a young age that if you wanted to play a sport, you needed to learn to deal with the criticisms. Some people feed off of others' failures. In order to prevail, you need to be strong enough, and you need to believe you will succeed.

I was even more ready for game two of the series. After the tough loss, we had to get ourselves together. Coach Josh switched up the defense and had Joe guard John, which seemed counterintuitive because all the Mobilio boys are short. However, what the Mobilio boys lack in height, we have in heart. We can guard anyone, and that's what Joe did.

The game was intense, and the fans were cheering for us. Despite the fervor, I was passive during the first quarter. I was thinking too much, and I didn't want to let my team down. Our team was at the line, shooting free throws, and Coach called me over. "Why aren't you shooting?"

"I don't want to miss."

"Shawn, you shoot. That's what shooters do. You're a shooter."

The score was tied at the end of the first quarter, 15-15. The B squad came in, and Mikey was on fire. He hit three threes. We were going crazy on the bench because little "Meatball" put us up by two. He wasn't the fastest, but he could shoot. The place was going crazy because of Mikey. After the half, we were up by six points, and John had four fouls. This meant he was close to fouling out. Team Rotary was behind for the first time in years. Coach huddled us up. "Attack the hoop, and make him foul you. We want him out of this game. If he fouls out, we will win." It felt like this was our time. Coach Josh drew up a new play. Because we were ready to inbound the ball, he designed it so one player would be out of bounds to catch a pass from someone inbounds, while the original inbounder ran down the court to catch a pass for a layup. The play worked perfectly. We felt like we couldn't lose this game with Coach Josh at the helm.

With just three minutes left, we were up by three points. Our opponents looked nervous. John was still in the game and started attacking the hoop, scoring two points. When we took the ball out, John stole it and scored again. We took the ball back once more and took it down court. I was open and in the same spot I had missed from the previous game. Joe knowingly passed me the ball, and I let it go. Nothing but net! Team Image was leading by two points. Rotary was forced to call a time-out. The spectators were going wild. My brothers hugged me as we went to the huddle. We were pumped, but I knew we hadn't won yet. There was still about a minute left. Coach said, "You know he's going to the basket. Joe, take a charge when he comes in."

Rotary inbounded the ball. Not surprisingly, John took it the full length of the court and drove right at Joe. Joe stood still, took a charge, and flew back into the wall as John made a layup. There was a pause as we waited to see whether the referee was going to call this a charge or a foul. It was a big turning point in the game. This call would determine whether we lost or advanced to game three. The ref put his hand behind his head to indicate that he was calling a charge on John. It was his fifth foul. He was out of the game. Coach's plan worked again!

With just twenty seconds left, we had possession. We knew it was time to hold the ball and make free throws. The ball was passed in, and I was fouled. I glanced at Coach before going up to he line, and he called me over. "See why I made you make twenty in a row? If you make two in a ow now, we win. You can do this, Shawn." Fans were screaming, John was on the bench glaring, oe and Mike were watching, and my mom was cheering in the stands. The pressure was on. I had practiced for this moment. This was my time to prove to my team that I belonged on the A squad despite my young age. The first throw went up and right in. The crowd was even wilder. I took my second shot. The ball left my hand awkwardly, and I missed.

Rotary got the rebound and called a time-out. I was disappointed because this meant they had a chance to tie the game with a three-pointer. We put on a full-court press. When the ball was inbounded, I ran by another defender, almost knocking him over. Rotary moved the ball up court and passed to the corner. One of their players was wide open, and he took the shot. The gymnasium went silent. Everyone watched as the ball soared up in the air, hit the front rim, and bounced out. Team Image won game two! We stormed the court like we had just won the national championship.

The celebration continued as we ran into the locker room. Coach's brother followed us in to congratulate us. He told us that he had never seen anything like that. "You guys are amazing! Good job!" he said. Coach was quiet for a second because he was crying. He was so shocked and happy with our team and the players.

The series was tied 1-1. Coach Josh grabbed the three brothers in a headlock and hugged us. The joyous feeling was surreal and unexplainable. It was a goose bump-worthy moment—we had our coach, and our coach had the three Mobilios.

At night, we liked a cold bedroom. Even if it was freezing outside, we had our window open with a fan to blow in cold air. Maybe it was the best way for us to cool off, especially after a hard-fought game. That night as I was lying in my bunk bed, looking up at the glow in the dark stars on our ceiling, I prayed for my family, friends, and Coach Josh. I really wanted to win game three—not just for us, but also for him. He brought so much passion to coaching, and he deserved to win.

"Goodnight, Meatball," I called down.

Mike kicked the bunk. "Shut up!"

"Goodnight, Mr. Charge who won the game," I said over to Joe.

"Shut up. I'm sleeping," was his response.

When we walked into the gym for game three, I noticed that John looked incredibly focused. After warm-up, the five starters from each team took the court. From the tip-off, it was all John. He was unstoppable. It was like playing against an NBA player. He was on a mission to win this game. By halftime, we were down twenty points.

Coach Josh brought us in and yelled at us. "Is this all you have, guys?" Evidently, it was all we had, and it wasn't enough. We came out fighting, and John went for thirty points.

After the game, we shook hands on the line. John and his father came up to my brothers and congratulated all three of us. Even though our team lost the championship series, the three of us gained respect within the league and the town. We were the first team to beat Team Rotary.

Coach Josh composed himself and told us he was proud of us. "Sometimes life doesn't go your way, but you should all stand tall and remember this lesson. Work harder and always remember to believe in yourselves."

PART 2

HIGH SCHOOL

Chapter 5

Greyhounds

It was the night before tryouts, and I couldn't sleep. The stars on the ceiling helped me focus my nerves and excitement. I already knew what I was going to wear because I was organized, and I had it all set out for the next day. Joe had tryouts for the varsity and junior varsity teams. I was only a freshman and expected to be on the freshmen team for Naugatuck High School with our pal, Coach Josh Ruccio. However, the varsity coach wanted me try out for the junior varsity and varsity teams. I was thrilled.

The next morning as part of the tryout, I did a one-on-one drill with Naugatuck High School's top senior shooting guard. I'd known him since childhood. He could shoot the lights out. As we drilled, I guarded him hard and didn't back down. When basketball players play defense, most don't play 100 percent, especially during practice. I gave everything I had because I knew if I didn't, I would be riding the bench. My height hadn't changed much, and I still had something to prove. I made a few stops and scored some baskets, and the coaches and players watching were shocked. The senior guard noticed the attention I was getting and bumped me, probably because I was making him look bad. He gave me a look of disgust and mumbled, "Chill out. This isn't the

NBA." Little did he know I had been playing in my own version of the NBA finals every morning at the park.

After tryouts, I went back to the locker room. Coach Josh approached me and said, "Good job, Shawn. Keep playing hard." I was proud of myself.

My mother picked us up and asked how tryouts went. Joe and I both told her it went well. Before we left for the day, we had heard a lot of guys talking trash. I knew my brother had my back, so it helped having him there. One of the lessons I learned through playing basketball was that sometimes you just have to be strong enough mentally to bypass negative people. I believe that you attract what you think. My brother and I both played hard during tryouts, so we focused on our performance.

The next day, the list of who made the teams was posted. I was on all three lists! As I wiped a tear from my eye, my brother slapped me on the head and said, "Good job, bro." As a freshman, I would play on all three team levels, even though Coach Josh had pushed for me to play for him. I was ready for the challenge.

High school was a lot different than middle school. I had to study a lot more. If I didn't have the grades, I wouldn't be eligible to play any sports. I played football in the fall and basketball in the winter. Now that I had three practices after school, I then went home to eat and study. This rigorous schedule took some adjustment. After the first week, my legs were very sore. My brain was tired. I didn't have the free time to practice on my own like I was used to. My freshmen teammates were cool, but they also had some resentment toward me because I played on the other two teams, and they didn't. Even though I could feel this animosity coming at me, I paid no mind to it. My goal was to play college basketball, and I needed to succeed in the classroom and on the hardwood.

I loved the game, and more importantly, I loved when I played. It helped me feel free with no worries, like an eagle flying high in an empty sky. There are biblical mentions of God as a lion and also an eagle. The eagle soars above all, something humans cannot do. And the lion is the king of the jungle. Each time I stepped onto the court, I felt like both a lion and an eagle.

Before the first freshmen game, I walked into the gym before anyone was there. There was a greyhound in the middle of the court. The peace and quiet of the gym allowed me to visualize myself playing and what I hoped to do to win that day. During my visualization, I confirmed I could do this. Tears came to my eyes because I was so proud of how hard I had worked. All the long hours in the gym and outside in the heat and snow were paying off. Playing basketball was what made me happy. Whether the competition was good or bad, it didn't matter—it was basketball.

My jersey number was fourteen. This was a trend in our family for all three of us to wear this number because our mom's birthday was on the fourteenth. It was a way for us to recognize all the hard work she did by bringing us to games and practices and the long hours she endured watching and cheering for us. We owed it to her to show our appreciation. I put on my jersey, laced up my shoes, and took a knee to pray to God. I thanked Him for this opportunity to play the game. As I walked down the hallway under the gymnasium, I saw the coaches talking in the office. I gave them a nod with an "eye of the tiger" look. My heart began to pound the closer I got to the court. I swung the door open, the clock was on, and it was show time.

Coach Josh looked at me and said, "You ready?"

"I was born ready, baby," I told him.

After tip-off, we were rolling. I was on fire, taking the ball to the basket, shooting, and making great passes. We won our first game. Coach Josh was happy, and so was I.

As I ran downstairs to put on my JV uniform, the team was already warming up. I had to hustle to join in. The JV coach brought us into a huddle and announced the starting lineup. I was not in it. Ouch. This was the first time in my life I wasn't starting. Sitting on the bench brought different tears to my eyes, and I asked myself why this was happening. I was the kind of kid who liked to prove people wrong when I was slighted, so maybe I made someone angry. However, I felt like I should have been playing because I knew I was better. I looked behind me and saw Joe and our family friend, Dan Bolton, watching. Joe gave me a sympathetic nod.

Halftime hit and I still wasn't playing. I was frustrated entering the locker room. We were down eight points to Watertown High School. The JV coach gave a speech that outlined a new game plan. When he finished, I asked to speak with him. He was a yelling type of coach, and I wasn't looking for trouble, but I wanted to know if I did something wrong. He told me I hadn't, but I should just be ready. He brushed my head with his hand, and that was it. While we were walking back up, it felt like he was going to put me in.

Throughout the third quarter, I was still on the bench. It was torture. My heart was pounding out of my chest. Most freshmen would be happy to be on the bench but not me. At the beginning of the fourth quarter, we trailed by ten. I started to lose hope. My mind was racing with thoughts. "Am I not good enough to be here? Are they that much better than I am? What's this coach's problem?" The horn went off, and Watertown had won. We traipsed back to the locker room. It was hard to pick up my head because I was feeling so hurt. The coach patted my back and told me to stay ready. I wanted to tell him to buzz off, but I stayed quiet. He gave us an after-game talk that I ignored.

I walked out the back door and bumped into Coach Josh. He was surprised when I completely broke down in his arms, crying like a baby. "Don't give up, Shawn. You have more heart than those guys. Come back to practice tomorrow and keep working," he told me. It felt like he truly believed in me. But I was still crushed. I couldn't even stay to watch the varsity game. Walking home, I took the trail in the back of the school because it was a shortcut to my house. I went straight to my bed without even showering. As I lay there, I thought about Coach Josh's encouragement, and he was right. I was not a quitter. I was going to show them my heart.

The next day, I was told to practice with the JV and varsity teams. That was fine. I preferred that. In order to be a starter, I would need to show the coaches that I was better than my teammates. Coach Josh stuck around to watch. We were spilt up on the court with JV on one side and varsity on the other. I was assigned to guard the point guard and played defense so hard, I could smell his gum. Steal after steal, basket after basket, I was all over my teammates. During the sprints, I was first. No one was outworking me. No one. A few older guys told me to chill out because this was only practice. In my head, I knew this was my chance to obtain my goals. After practice, the JV coach once again patted me on the back, but this time he told me I did a good job. Coach Josh smirked at me from the bleachers. These coaches and players were not going to dictate my future.

For the second JV game, the coach kept the same starting five. This added fuel to my fire. If I was substituted in, it would be my time to show them I belonged. The first quarter ended, and we were down by five points. Coach said, "Mobilio, you're in."

I jumped off the bench, ran to the scorer's table, and loudly announced my name. "Mobilio checking in!" They must have thought I was nuts. I was too excited to play to notice. I brought the ball up and ran the offense. Next, I set a screen on the block, popped up, and forced myself open. The ball was passed to me, and I took the jump shot. When I let go of the ball, it had enough backspin to knock someone out—nothing but net. It was my first basket as a JV player. I switched to defense and got a steal. Running the ball to the basket, I made the layup and was fouled. The fans in the Naugatuck gymnasium were waking up. There was a flow of energy from the fans to me, the freshman point guard. We won the game, and I could hear people saying, "Who is that freshman?"

Coach Josh was a little mad at me because I was not playing on the freshmen team anymore. Even though I loved him, my eyes were set on playing varsity. The only problem was that the starting point guard was my older brother, and the other guard was the coach's son. Man, talk about an uphill climb! I was in a pickle because I didn't want to compete against my brother for the same position. I worked hard every practice, but I didn't play on varsity. As the starting point guard on JV, I averaged the most points and assists on the team.

After the JV game, I warmed up with the varsity team, knowing I'd be sitting on the bench. We were playing Wolcott High School, and it was a big game. We needed to win it. In the fourth quarter, the varsity coach came down to the end of the bench and called out my name. He was putting me in for his son. As I walked on the court, I looked around the packed stands. My fellow JV teammates were watching me from the bench. My brother was on the floor. He smiled at me and told me to stay with number twelve because he's fast. He instructed me to just play defense, so I stuck to number twelve like glue. I actually stole the ball from him and made a layup for two points. When the game clock buzzed, we had won. Everyone was smiling, including my JV coach. It was nice to be on the court again with my brother like old times! We just need Mikey to get into high school so it could be the three of us once again. I received a lot of encouragement, and it felt good to be welcomed. My extended family was at the game, and it was nice to have their support. Walking down to the locker room, Coach Josh said to me, "All heart."

The season seemed to fly by. After the last game, there was a meeting with the coaches for al three basketball teams. As I walked in, the JV coach asked me if I was leaving.

"Who said that?" I asked.

"Rumors are going around that your transferring," he replied.

I told him that I wasn't but truthfully, I wasn't happy with the coaching staff. I didn't like the way they were treating Joe and favoring the varsity coach's son. Both were juniors, and I couldn' sit behind that.

At the end of the school year, I decided to leave. My father asked me to work for him over the summer, and it was a lot more convenient to stay at his house. Luckily, my mother understood, and I was with her every weekend. Mike wanted to come too, so he moved with me. We would both attend Seymour High School in the fall. Joe would stay with our mom and finish his senior year at Naugatuck High School.

If opportunity doesn't knock, you need to build a door and bust through.

Chapter 6

Wildcats

Leaving my friends was not easy, and I knew opposing my teammates would be difficult. I was aware that at some point my new school would compete against my old school, which would mean I would be head-to-head with Joe. As I walked into my first period class at Seymour High School, I recognized a kid I played against last year. We immediately hit it off, and I was frequently invited to his house. His family remembered me as the kid who hit the floor hard and yelled, "Defense!" They were happy I was on their team. Bobby and his family were amazing people and welcomed my family; we were grateful for their friendship. They told us about a program for strengthening and conditioning run by a teacher in the school named Coach Demarco. Even though I was playing football, I signed up and also signed up Mikey. We attended the tough, twice per week workouts, and the coach noticed the effort we put in. He caught a glimpse of the Mobilio work ethic.

As time went by, Coach D invited the head varsity coach to come see us workout. The coach liked what he saw and spoke to us after one of the workouts. I told him we came from Naugatuck, and we were interested in trying out. At that time, I don't think the coach knew what he had in front of him. Here were two kids willing to give 100 percent every day. In order to stay in basketball shape, Mike and I would go to courts in Naugatuck and Waterbury to play pickup basketball as often as we could. Seymour didn't have much competition in their division, but when we showed up, we made sure everyone had to work. That's the beauty of hard work—when you do it, everyone has to step up their game, or they will be left behind.

I didn't sleep the night before tryouts. This seemed to be a pattern for me. My father put a basketball hoop in the driveway for us, so I was outside most of the night shooting. Even though he never drilled with us, it was great to have his support. With my cd player in my pocket and the stars shining brightly, I worked hard during that midnight practice.

The tryouts were after school, and the only guy I knew was Bobby. He was a good athlete and a solid basketball player. It seemed like a few of the guys on the team weren't too happy when I introduced myself to them. I could even see them sizing me up, judging me because I was shorter than all of them. Nothing changes when it comes to competition! The buzz was around, and the juniors didn't want a sophomore taking up their varsity time. Little did they know, I played more as a freshman than they did as sophomores. I decided to keep to myself. This wasn't the first time I had switched schools, and I knew it could be a lonely road. Learning to block out people helped me focus on my task. The point guard on the team was a junior. He was about my height and during the tryouts, I played him so hard, he kept losing the ball. In frustration, he swore and yelled and lost control. It became physical, and every one of those juniors came at me. Even though there were five or six of them trying to make me look bad, I loved the challenge. I made every one of them look foolish. These guys all knew each other and had played together since childhood. I understood that they were all best friends, but this was a game. They were meeting up with a real basketball player. The coach was happy with me. Winners don't make excuses—they play through it.

I learned I had made the JV team but would probably play a bit on the varsity team. That wasn't the result I wanted. Mike also made the JV team. At practices, I played hard every day. My teammates were prone to a lot of moaning and whining. But I kept doing what I did best, and that was to play the game at 100 percent. To get more practice time, I would hide a ball behind he bleachers and walk out the front with Mike. After the coaches left the gym, we would sneak back in to shoot for another hour. We did this for three years, and the janitors eventually were used to us doing it. Mikey and I would get in the gym as much as we could. While the others were going home, we would still be practicing. And we were improving because of it.

The place was packed at our first game. Seymour fans squeezed into the small gym, and they knew how to get loud quickly. Gold and yellow streamers were all over the walls with WILDCATS painted across the floor. The coach had me start for the JV game and sit during the varsity game. After every JV game, I would suit up for the varsity game, just as I had at Naugatuck.

The varsity coach had his starting five sit on the bench. The problem with his lineup was that wasn't in it. When a coach does this, and a player is not ready for the competition, I understand. But if the player is ready and not getting a fair opportunity, I call this politics. I had to fight this, and there was only one way to beat politics. I needed to shine so bright that the coach had no choice but to start me.

After the first varsity game, which I didn't play in, the juniors were smiling as they walked off the court. We had lost the game, and they were smiling at me. How could they be smiling? I was pissed off that we lost and didn't get a chance to play. I made sure the coach saw it in my eyes when I saw him in his office after the game. As I walked out of the locker room and through the gym to walk home, a parent walked up to me and said, "You shouldn't even be on the court. You're a sophomore. My kid didn't even suit up as a sophomore." I didn't say anything. Instead, walked to the weight room, put my headphones on, and began to lift. I was so mad that I bench pressed as much as I could for as many times as I could until my arms gave out. As a young kid, I realized that I was on my own and that I had to work hard in order to succeed. No one was going to give me anything for free. I needed to take it.

I was the first one in the locker room for practice the next day. When I went on the court to warm up, I had my headphones on and started shooting around. A few of the juniors walked by to go to the locker room, and I could hear them say, "Look at this guy trying to show us up. He still won't play." This was music to my ears. It fueled my determination to be better in school and on the court. And I could prove it through my actions. One day, coach called us into the locker room He started by addressing the negative energy in the room. In front of everyone, he said something that I will never forget. "Guys, Shawn's a sophomore, but he is going to play." The faces of the upperclassmen dropped. Inside my head, I was celebrating. "It's about time coach! Let's win some games!" It seemed like I had overcome the politics by using hard work.

During this time, my relationship with God grounded me. He helped me get through those adversarial situations. Instead of reacting when things went wrong, I prayed to God and asked Him to make things okay. It is easy to fight someone. It's hard to not fight back. If you work hard and do things correctly, your time will come.

It was also helpful that my parents made time to attend games when they could, especially my mom who had to drive further. Having their support for my dream was important to me.

Imagine my surprise when at the next game, I wasn't in the starting lineup again. However, on this night, I felt like things were going to change. Maybe those fans would be jumping for me!

The starting point guard on our team wasn't good with pressure from the stronger inner city teams. But I was, and this was my chance.

The coach called me in, and the announcer said, "Shawn Mobilio checks into the game." I tucked my shirt in and wiped my feet for grip. Walking past my teammates, I thought, "None of you are actually basketball players. I have to make you basketball players now." Good leaders make everyone around them stronger. Whether I liked them or not, my goal was to demonstrate some true leadership and make them better. Of course, I also needed to shoot the ball well. If I brought my energy out onto the court, it would excite the crowd, even if they didn't like me. Everyone likes winning. I brought the ball up, and I stepped over the yellow line, a little over from the half-court line. Then I took the shot. I didn't care—I needed to make a statement. My shot was all net, and the place went nuts. Next, I began breaking down the defense by making no-look passes to my teammates. The three-point line was my domain. The fans and coaches were witnessing something special. In the end, Seymour beat Kennedy High School. The headline in the newspaper the next day said, "Mobilio leads the way for Seymour."

I received a phone call from my friend Dan, who told me he was coming to my next game. It was against Naugatuck High School. Joe was the point guard for their team, and this was the first time we would be playing against each other competitively. The day I knew would happen was here. I was nervous. We played our whole lives with each other, and we knew each other's moves. The idea of competing against one of my brothers presented a mental challenge that was hard to explain. During the game, Joe was roasting our junior point guard. I was put in to guard my brother because he was making our guy look bad. Coach called a time-out with forty seconds left in the game. We were down by two points. The coach from Naugatuck thought the game was in the bag. The clock was ticking, and we were setting up an offense. Our shooting guard, who had the most awkward shot I'd ever seen, was designated to hit the shot. As I crossed half court, I recognized the play wasn't working. He was kind of open, but I didn't want him to shoot the ball.

Taking a chance while I was deep, I shot the ball with a high arc. The place was silent when the ball was in the air. It came down perfectly into the net. With eight seconds remaining, Naugatuck called a time-out. My teammates were hugging me. I was a little shocked to receive this kind of affection, but like I said, everyone loves a winner. Naugatuck inbounded the ball and took a shot. It was no good, and we won. As I was going down the handshake line, I saw Dan walking out of the gym, shaking his head and smiling.

Our team made it to the state tournament that year but lost in the second round. I led the way for Seymour. In the spring, I added track to my schedule. I thought that speed running would be beneficial to my basketball game.

My junior year was kind of a blur. I was really inspired by my football coach. He solidified my commitment to having a strong work ethic and mental toughness. His dedication to football was equal to my dedication to basketball. Academically, I was not a great student. Attendance wasn't an issue; completing homework was. Mikey and I played on the same team. He was the bench guy who would come in when I was taken out. Joe had graduated from Naugatuck, so we didn't compete against him. Our team made it to the state championship again. College coaches were taking notice of me. Bobby's mother paid attention to this and insisted I take the SATs in preparation for college. She even paid for me to take the test. Because I wasn't a good student and didn't understand the value of the SATs, I didn't score well. To me, academics were not important. It was basketball that was going to get me into college, not my grades and test results. There weren't any teachers guiding me or talking to me about my future. We all just made sure my grades were high enough to play. My destiny to play college basketball was in my hands, as long as I continued to work hard on my game.

During my senior year, Bob and I were made captains of the team. Despite playing hard and doing the best we could, it wasn't in the cards to make states that year. But we were a unified team, and I made sure that any good player in any grade was welcomed on the Seymour basketball team. My grandmother taught us manners and insisted that we treat people nicely. It was important to her that we have a good heart, and I tried to pass this along to my teammates.

It was nice to be recognized and receive awards because it was my final year of high school. I received All Conference, All Valley, and All Suburban honors, and an honorable mention for the All-State team in 2006. Scouts and recruiters for colleges continued to show interest in me and would ask to speak with me after games. One college was really interested, and they called me all the time. That college was Western Connecticut State University.

Chapter 7

Rejection

My only dream was to play basketball in college. That was the goal, and it was time to apply.
I met with the head coach and his assistant coach at Western Connecticut State University, a
NCAA Division III school. The coach and members of his team were heavily recruiting me. This
seemed like a no brainer because it was close to my dad's house, they wanted me, and I wanted to
play college ball. I didn't think about looking at other schools. The varsity coach had brought me
to Western for a small tour, and it seemed fine to me. I simply applied to Western Connecticut,
and I was going to college.

My father didn't want me to go to college. He owned a heating and cooling company with his
brothers and sister called Anthony's Fuel, and he wanted me to stay home and work in the family
business. This is what Joe did after high school, so that was the expectation for me. I agreed to
work for him during the summer months, but this was not what I wanted to do for a living. I was
meant to play basketball and go to college.

As my senior year of high school was winding down, I was outside shooting around, waiting
for the mail to come. *Swish*, a shot went in just as the postman pulled up. Before he could put the
mail in our box, my hand was ready to intercept. I saw an envelope with Western Connecticut
State University on it. I grabbed it, ran to my room, and slammed the door saying to myself, "This
is it, baby!"

The letter said:

Dear Mr. Shawn Mobilio,

The admissions committee has carefully reviewed your application to the University of Western Connecticut State University. After much consideration, I regret to inform you that we are unable to offer you a place in the class of 2010.

"Why me?" I cried as I fell to my knees. The coach had promised me a spot, hadn't he? So, what happened? Wiping my tears, I grabbed the phone and called the head coach. When he answered, I asked him about my rejection from the school. My grades were not good enough, and my SAT scores were too low, he indicated. I couldn't understand why that mattered. My basketball playing was exceptional. Though I was still stunned, I thought to ask him about what I should do now. He suggested I attend a community college for a year to prove that I could handle the academic work and then transfer in.

I hung the phone up and wept. This wasn't the plan, and it wasn't the way I wanted it to go. I thought about all my heroes growing up: my mom, Coach Josh, my dad, my brothers. They would be so disappointed. I thought about my basketball idols: Michael Jordan and Lebron James. I just wanted to be like them. The pain of defeat was back, and this time I was done with basketball.

That night, I shared the news with my father. "Wake up bright and early tomorrow, and we will start working." Joe looked over and nodded his approval, so I agreed to my dad's plan. I packed all my basketball pictures, game stuff, and trophies in a box and threw it under my bed. Maybe everyone was right about me. I was too short. I would never play college basketball.

As young kids, my brothers and I grew up learning karate. I started boxing when I was sixteen. Both karate and boxing were a way for us to get out our energy when we couldn't play basketball. Now that I wasn't going to play anymore, I felt the need to box again. I hadn't boxed since moving to Seymour. And I had never boxed competitively. I wanted to get in the ring. This would be the outlet I needed to work out my anger.

There was a gym in Bridgeport that I knew about, so I went there. After a few visits, I found a boxing coach, an ex-marine named Marcello, and he took me under his wing. Marcello and I trained eight hours a day. I learned a lot as we trained like marines. He was incredibly disciplined like me, and I soaked up every minute of it. Marcello was crazy, but I loved him. He understood my frustrations and enjoyed training with me. We were the same Italian and Portuguese fighting men. Training took my mind off of basketball. I trained like I was a professional looking for my next million dollar fight. At the same time, I also worked my full-time job.

Marcello set me up to work with Coach John, a former professional boxer and MMA professional fighter, for extra training. Coach John had me fight against professionals during our sessions at his gym, so when it came to fighting amateurs, it was easy.

I trained hard for six months and had over fifty sparring matches with amateur and professional fighters. My first amateur fight was in Waterbury at a titanium boxing facility that was ninety-eight degrees. It was against an MMA fighter who had won eight matches and had never lost. He was twenty-nine years old, and he was just over six feet tall. I had no fights on record in the USA Boxing book because my experience thus far had been in sparring. As I was introduced, I could hear my family cheering from the stands. My good friend, Joe, was there too. We had met through our love of boxing. He held up a speaker that was blasting *Eye of Tiger* as I ntered the ring. In my corner, I had a flashback to my college rejection letter. I said to myself, "This guy is going to pay for that now. Sorry!"

We walked up to each other in the middle of the ring. My opponent looked at me and said, "I'm going to knock you out."

"That's not nice," I thought to myself, but I didn't care to say anything back.

The bell rang, and he attacked me like I had stolen his wallet. He was throwing all sorts of crazy punches. I slipped in a jab and threw a straight right-hand punch that met his nose. There was an audible loud pop. The crowd reacted and from that punch on, I kept jabbing him. He bounced all over the place, but I refused to relent. We combated each other, round after round. I continued to fight hard, right up to the end when my opponent succumbed. After the last bell, I threw my arms toward my trainer, yelling at him to take my gloves off because they felt like bricks. It was announced that I was the winner. The referee raised my hand, and I had officially won my first match and was undefeated.

The daily grind of work was hard for me. My Uncle Anthony was my ride to work every day. He was an early morning riser and driven, just like the rest of the family. Each morning, he picked me up at 5:00 a.m. There were days I missed my alarm clock and woke up to a phone call from Uncle Anthony asking where I was. It was hard to explain to him that I had just graduated high school and wasn't used to this lifestyle. When I asked him why we had to get to work so early, he would answer with some quip about an early bird getting a worm. Our routine included going into the office to complete all the administrative work before we would go on the road to do calls. My brother, Joe, would ride with my dad and meet us at the job. They started later than we did, which hardly seemed fair. Some days, I didn't get home from work until after 8:00 p.m. Mikey was still in high school, so he didn't have to endure this new reality of mine.

I was trying to transition my brain from playing basketball to becoming a working man. My uncle knew what had happened and tried to give advice. "Shawn, you can't ride with your basketball to work. You have to work hard and put the ball down." Once, we were in a basement working on an oil cleaning and filter change, and I saw a basketball in the corner. Without thinking, I started breaking out my moves. My uncle scolded me. "Cut it out! Basketball is over. Now get back to work." Even though I was working hard and boxing in my free time, basketball was chasing me. I thought I could leave it behind by hiding it in boxes under my bed. There wasn't a day that went by that I didn't think about it.

There was a time, about four months after graduation, when I stopped down to play a pickup game with my brothers and our family friend, Dan. I was out of basketball shape, but I could still play. My duo lost. Dan yelled, "Shawn, you suck! What happened to you? You can barely dribble." I told him I quit basketball, I was working full time, and I was becoming a boxer. He looked directly at me, and I'll never forget what he said. "You have your whole life to work, Shawn. Go to school, play basketball, and you can make this a living." Dan had told me before to keep going and work toward my dream. His advice was lost in my rejection grief.

At some point, Dan's words began to swim around in my head. Those phrases, "You suck! What happened to you?" really bothered me. Grabbing a ball from under my bed, I went outside to shoot in the dark with my headphones on. Thoughts of playing college basketball overtook the negativity. It felt so natural and so right to me. Even though my body was sore from working all day, and my hands were sore from boxing, running drills and shooting baskets helped me feel like myself again. With darkness all around me, I prayed, "God, I really want to play and go back to school." I completed the prayer, opened my eyes, and a shooting star flew over me. At that moment, I knew it was meant to be. I needed to go back to school. Waking up my father, I announced, "I'm going to college." He rolled over and said we would talk about it in the morning.

It was hard to sleep that night. When I woke up in the morning, I told my father again about my plan to go to college. His response was, "If you go to school, you are on your own. I am not paying for your school bills, and it will take you your whole life to pay them back if you take out loans." My mother was very supportive of my decision but obviously not my father. I didn't care. The decision was already made in my mind.

I called the head coach at Western Connecticut State University to tell him my news. The plan was to start at a community college in Waterbury and get good grades. I could save enough money to take one semester there. After that semester, I would transfer to WCSU and play basketball.

PART 3

COLLEGE

Chapter 8

New Plan

Initially, everything worked as I had planned. Before my classes at community college, I went to the local YMCA in Waterbury to train four hours a day. I practiced ball handling, lifted weights, and swam laps in the pool. It was good for me because most of the guys at the YMCA were Division I or Division II basketball players. It made me better. My efforts at the YMCA were preparing me for competition.

My GPA at the end of the semester was a 2.8. The WCSU head coach was thrilled and told me I would definitely be accepted as a transfer student. One of the local coaches, Coach Parker who was at University of Bridgeport, listened to my plan to transfer. He advised me to check out Division II schools. According to him, Southern Connecticut State University was looking for guys, and I might be able to walk onto the team. This was a potential opportunity that I hadn't thought of, and I should explore it.

There wasn't much time for me to take a tour of Southern Connecticut, so I went with my gut instinct. I decided to apply to both WCSU and SCSU. The result was that I was accepted at both schools! My gut then told me to take a risk and attend SCSU in New Haven, Connecticut. I would major in physical education. When I told the coach at Western about my decision, he wasn't happy.

After I moved into my first dorm room, I walked over to Moore Field House where the gymnasium was located. This would be the first time I had ever seen a college basketball court. I opened the door and was amazed at how shiny that floor looked. I had never seen a gym look so shiny. There was a track encompassing the court with bleachers around the top of the gym. The lights hit the wood floor and made it stand out. The entire gym was empty except for me standing in the middle of it. I looked at the banners hanging and thought, "This is where I belong." Ironically, a nice gentleman informed me the gym was closed and kicked me out.

The athletic offices were upstairs, so I ventured up to see what they looked like. There was a waiting area but no administrative assistant. I walked around and saw about ten doors with signs for all different sports. As I came to the last one on the left, I saw a sign that said SCSU Men's Basketball. The door was closed, but I could hear someone in there. My hands were sweating, and I was nervous when I knocked on the door. A tall man with hair that was slickly gelled back answered the door. "Can I help you?"

"Hi, my name is Shawn Mobilio. I would like to try out for the basketball team here."

He emitted a short giggle and said, "Sorry, but you are too short to play at this level. Good luck!" Then he slammed the door in my face.

I was completely shocked. Not sure what to do, I walked across the street to the cafeteria. What do I have to do? Did I choose the wrong school?" I kept asking myself. As I strolled into the café with my basketball in one hand and my gym bag around my arm, I saw a table of about ten guys in the back corner. They all looked like basketball players. We made eye contact, but that was the extent of our interaction. One of them was lamenting, "I don't want to practice tomorrow at 5:30 a.m." I grabbed a glass of milk and formulated an idea that I thought might work. If I were to show up at the gym at 5:00 a.m. to shoot around, the coach would see me there and know that I was serious about being on the team. What else did I have to lose?

I continued to think about this plan while in line at the food station. One of the food workers who was randomly standing around interrupted my thoughts. "Hey, pal."

I said, "Do I know you?"

"I'm just saying hi."

We decided to sit together to eat. His name was Boo Slick. After introductions, we began to chat. I shared my situation with him. He was super encouraging and told me to go forward with my plan. Boo told me, "Real recognizes real." I truly believe God sends me angels and has done so my whole life. These angels are always positive. Boo was one of these angels for me. I left the cafeteria with increased confidence. As I walked through the field house, I glanced over at the court one last time and said, "I will see you in the morning."

My alarm went off at 4:30 a.m., but I was already up. There were no other college kids up this early. I wasn't the top recruit, I wasn't the biggest nor the tallest, but I knew when I made it on this team, I would outwork everyone. The players would be just rolling out of bed at 5:00 a.m. but I was already walking in the front door of the gym. The security guard at the door stopped me and asked if I played for the soccer team. Without hesitation, I told him I did. They must have practice at the same time, which worked to my favor. Clearly my height made him think I played soccer. Whatever I had to say in order to get in was what I was going to do. I just needed to be seen by the coach.

The court was empty. The feeling of being the first one in the gym and the last one out was so familiar to me. I put on my headphones and went straight to work for fifteen minutes. Two oaches were in the balcony watching, but I stayed focused on my task. They could watch me get

n my shots and make their judgments. I was there before everyone else, so I was the star of the

how.

The team began to stroll in, looking like they just came off of a rollercoaster ride. They

ppeared dizzy and frazzled. When the coaches came on the court, I stepped off. Blue blinders

eparated the court from the surrounding track, which meant you couldn't see from one to the

ther. I did a physical workout of running, push-ups, sit-ups, ball handling, and sprints while the

eam practiced. The coaches in the balcony could see me, but the players couldn't. Once practice

vas over, my plan was to go right back on the court and shoot for another hour.

This was my routine for one week. It was Friday morning, and I was beginning to lose hope.

he coaches saw me every day but never spoke to me. I completed my ball handling exercise

vith a tennis ball when the guy with slicked back hair walked over and introduced himself as the

ead coach. He invited me to come to practice the next morning. Controlling my emotions, I told

im I'd be there. I was walking out the back door, ready to jump up and down or cry tears of

appiness, when I heard him yell for me.

"We have a lot of paperwork to fill out. Meet me in my office today around lunch time."

I sprinted to my room and called all my family to tell them I was going to be playing Division

I basketball. They could hear how pumped I was. Dan and Coach Josh were also excited for me.

had trouble focusing in my morning classes because all I could think about was basketball. After

unch, I met with the coach and filled out the paperwork.

Saturday morning, I walked to the café before practice to eat a good meal. The team was

itting together. In an effort to connect with them, I walked over to sit in an empty chair at their table. One of the players grabbed the chair and put his foot on it. So that's how it was. "No big deal," I thought. "I can sit alone."

Boo Slick came over to join me and said, "I heard you're on the team."

"Yup! I start today."

"Yes! You got this," he enthusiastically responded. He also said, "Don't worry about those guys. They are just jealous of you."

"I'm used to it," I told him.

The team was walking over to the gym, and I followed behind them with my headphones on. Entering the locker room, I saw that each of the guys had his name on a locker. I didn't have a locker yet, so I put my stuff on the court.

The coaches came out and told us it was time to work. We did shooting drills, conditioning, and team offense. It was a little different for me because this was my first collegiate practice. What was the same was that I left it all on the court. In the back of my mind, I knew that as a walk-on, I could be cut at any time. Nothing was guaranteed. Most the guys were on scholarships so even though they worked hard, I wasn't convinced they gave 100 percent. I believe when you get to a certain level and you are comfortable, you become complacent. I made sure I was never settling, because I had something to prove. Playing basketball wasn't just for myself—I was playing for my family, friends, and fans back home. From the start of practice to the end, I gave it all I had. After practice, the team would go back to the café to eat. I could barely even drink because I was so tired. Every part of my body hurt when I was done.

Coach called a team meeting one morning to go over the rules and to introduce us to the athletic director. We sat down to listen, and it was a long meeting with tons of paperwork. I found he coach to be motivating. He told us we would be the hardest working team in the country. We walked into the locker room before practice, and there was a label on my locker that said "Shawn Mobilio." I smiled, put my stuff in the locker, and ran onto the court feeling awesome.

One of the point guards on the team was small like me. He was a solid player. He came from a top school in New York, and his team was featured in a game on ESPN. There were a lot of good guys on the team from all over. But I proved I could play with them and felt I could start over them. As I took my three pointers, I felt a high level of confidence.

Coach blew the whistle to end practice and told me to follow him to his office. I asked myself, "Is he going to make me the starting point guard?" My mood turned quickly when he told me to sit down. "Shawn, you have a 1.8 GPA. What have you been doing? You are ineligible to play through the NCAA Clearinghouse. You can no longer be on this team." My head dropped to my lap. "The only way I will take you back is if you have a 3.0 GPA."

I walked out of there stone-faced. My emotions were in check as I cleared out my locker and made my way back to my dorm room. I buzzed myself in, walked through the kitchen, and put my stuff on my bed. Then I entered the bathroom, locking the door behind me. Tears fell like a waterfall. My world was over. I worked so hard to get on that team, but I had only focused on basketball. I didn't do my schoolwork. Again. For eight hours, I stayed in the bathroom. My face looked like I was beaten up in the ring.

The one call I wasn't expecting was from my father. He was worried about me. I held it in and told him I was okay. During a long walk that night, a hundred things were going on in my head. All I could think about was that I failed myself. How was I going to make it right again? There was only one place to go and that was to church. I sat in a pew and spoke with God. I asked him to give me the strength to be strong. Basketball was my passion and my life. I needed to get my grades up to achieve my goal. Before I left, I told myself, "If I can get past this wall, I can get over any wall." It helped me to feel stronger. I actually went home that night and read one of my textbooks.

I started to study more than practice in the gym. I studied all day and played for only a few hours at night. Then I studied some more in the library. I asked for extra credit assignments from my teachers. For additional help, I stayed after or went into class early to go over things with my teachers. I was determined to get back on the team. Boo Slick and his friends in the café were my number one fans, along with my family and friends. Others thought I was crazy and told me to drop basketball. But they were wrong. This was my life, and I was going to get back on that team. Sometimes in life you need to work differently to follow your dreams.

Chapter 9

One Door Closes, Another Opens

My life had collapsed around me. I was kicked off the basketball team because I wasn't studying. If I truly wanted to achieve my dream, academics would have to be my priority. It was time to take a step back from my dreams. Little did I know that out of my greatest despair would come the greatest gift—a second chance.

Four months after being kicked off the team, my grades were improving. The studying, extra help, extra work, and focus helped me become a better student. My GPA was at 2.8. There was a final hurdle I needed to jump to end this semester with a 3.0 GPA. I had one more test for a class that was difficult for me. Macro Economics was a subject I just couldn't get into, mainly because it was so boring. I had to score an eighty percent or higher on the next test to reach my academic goal. This professor acted strangely when we took tests. They were administered in a huge lecture hall, and he would creep around the room looking for cheaters. One time, I looked back and he was hiding between three seats. It was hilarious to see the lengths this guy went to catch someone cheating but also distracting when you are trying to concentrate.

The test was given at 9:00 a.m. sharp. I studied many hours during the week and the night before. I had enough motivation and didn't need to drink coffee to keep me going. While I was grabbing an early breakfast, my fans in the café were all cheering for me because they knew this was a big day. The best part about it was that I was feeling confident. As I walked in the lecture hall, my professor was reading his newspaper, legs propped up with his ankles crossed. He looked like he had no worries in the world. I was sweating and trying to keep my wits about me, the weight of the moment sinking in. When the test was distributed, I went through it carefully, reading every question twice so I could answer each to the best of my ability.

The pressure was on to earn a grade of at least eighty percent. After completing the exam, I waited outside the lecture hall until everyone had left and continued to wait for about an hour before the professor came out. I explained my situation to him, and he agreed to meet me at his office in twenty minutes. Feeling too anxious to pace or go somewhere else, I just went to his office and sat outside his door. As he walked by me, he laughed and told me to follow him in. I was sweating profusely as I watched him go through my exam. This was the first time I had ever felt this level of nerves! With every "x" marked, my anxiety increased. He flipped to the last page, and my feet were involuntarily moving like I was listening to a rock song, tapping with the beat. With a red pen, he wrote "79%" with a circle around it. I held my breath and immediately pulled an extra credit assignment to give to him. Previously, he had told the class that if we emailed it or handed it in, we would receive two extra points on the final. He smiled and added the two points, making my final grade an eighty-one! I was so thrilled and thanked him for taking the time to correct my test early. He wished me luck as I left. After taking about ten steps down the hall, I realized I left my bag and test in his office. He was in the doorway holding my things when I returned. We laughed at my excitement and relief.

I ran to my room and called all my family and friends. Grades would be posted soon, which meant I could approach the coach and give him the good news too.

With my grades back up, I returned to my workouts and practice regime. The semester had ended, and I wanted to get into shape to be ready for the next season. Each morning, I would wake up at 4:30 a.m., and I would run the track. It brought me back to my high school days when I participated in track to make sure I wouldn't lose any speed in the off-season for basketball. Using the track early in the morning by myself was great. I was getting a head start on everyone

1 the world. The gate to the track was typically locked, so I would jump the fence to do my

workouts. I tried to incorporate long distance training, sprint workouts, agility, and bleachers.

Mixing up my routine was important. If I wasn't using a basketball for ball handling drills, I was

using a tennis ball. Some days, I would use two tennis balls and dribble them simultaneously. I

had a lot of freedom to do what I needed to do because no one was up that early, trying to kick

me out.

The basketball court was closed in the afternoons due to team practice. I would watch them

while sitting in the top balcony and write down all the workouts they did, including the five-man

drills. My goal was to replicate the drills on my own. When it came to the five-man drill, I put

trash cans in different spots all over the court. It's important to call out a name when making a

pass because communication is key. I may have looked like complete a fool, yelling at the trash

cans, but I didn't care. That's how much passion I had for improving my game. I was not going to

be left behind.

Grades were posted when I logged onto my account in the library (I didn't have a laptop in

college). My GPA was a 3.1. "Wahoo!" I yelled. The librarian and other patrons looked at me

like they wanted to throw a book at me. My excitement was quickly extinguished when I realized

had left my ID back in my room and couldn't print. I needed to have a hard copy of my grades

to show the coach. It took me three minutes to run and retrieve what I needed. It was a comedy of

errors when I returned to the library, as the printer was out of paper. Finally achieving success for

this simple task, I ran to the field house and up to the coach's door. The administrative assistant

was my next roadblock because she made me wait to see the coach. Sitting around for what

seemed like hours, she finally allowed me back to his office.

As I walked in, the coach yelled, "Mobilio!" I handed him the copy of my final grades. "Wow! Incredible work on improving your grades! This shows me you really want to be on the team."

"Coach, you wanted a 3.0. Well, I gave you a 3.1."

"I see that! Great job. You're back on the team."

This was an amazing feeling. I literally skipped back to my dorm room to call everyone and tell them the great news!

The next morning, I was excited to join the individual workouts. I just needed the schedule. Thinking the coach would let me know when he wanted me to attend, I ran into his office. It was completely empty. Totally cleaned out. The logical explanation was that the offices were being renovated, so I found the athletic director's office to ask her where the basketball coaches were relocated. The response stopped me in my tracks. She informed me they were no longer with the school. I was at a loss for words. Something must have happened, and they were gone. Was all my hard work for nothing?

I asked myself, "What am I doing here?" Dan was always great at talking things out with me so I called him and told him what happened. He told me to keep working hard and never give up. But I was beginning to lose faith.

The best thing about this time was that I had the right people around me. My circle of family and friends would not let me give up. That's what is important in life—knowing who the right people are and having them around you. Their support was important to me because I needed to keep working toward my end goal. No one else was going to do it for me.

With a new coach coming in, several teammates indicated they were going to transfer. It's common for incoming coaches to bring players with them from their previous teams. Some didn't want to get involved with that. I felt that I had to meet this new head coach, even though many were telling me to leave. All I needed to do was show this coach my hard work and talent. The former coach hadn't officially re-instated me on the roster, so I was not allowed to participate in the individual workouts.

After the new coach arrived, I knew I had to impress him. I dressed in a shirt and tie and brought my resume in a folder. After the workout, I approached the coach, told him my story, and handed him my folder. He told me I could try out in the fall. It seemed like he was going to give me a fair shot. He even gave me a packet of workouts to do over the summer.

I made sure to follow everything in that packet every day with no days off. If I was going to make this team, I needed to do all I could to put me ahead of the others. Each morning, I woke up early and made 500 jump shots, including layups. As my dad pulled out of the driveway for work at 5:00 in the morning, he saw me shooting outside. He really didn't know what to say. But he recognized that his eighteen-year-old son was fighting for his dreams. Most people thought I was crazy because the odds were against me. They thought it was nearly impossible for me to play at the college or professional level. But others challenged that position and asked why I couldn't. This was most in-line with my thinking. College and professional athletes are human like everyone else and have their own unique journey to pursue. The qualities that are most important to be a great athlete is hard work and heart. You can have all the talent in the world but if you don't work hard, you're wasting that talent, and someone else is going to take that spot.

School was back in session, and I called the coach to find out when the tryouts would take place. He hadn't scheduled them yet, so he said he would contact me in a few days. Even though I tried to be patient, I still showed up at his office to ask in person. He explained to me that he would reach out via email and took my contact information. Weeks went by, and I didn't hear from him. I put my head down and continued to work hard on and off the court. The buzz around school was that preseason was beginning in just two weeks, and I still hadn't received a call or email. Another week went by, and I still heard nothing! Now my patience was thin, so I called th coach. He told me to come down for a tryout two days before preseason.

The tryout was in the style of a pickup game. I played hard and felt like it was a great day. After, the coach called me up to his office to meet with him and the assistant coach.

"Shawn, close the door."

I didn't really know what to think. Was this another rejection or the accomplishment I've been waiting for my whole life?

He looked at me and said, "You had the best tryout out of all the walk-ons, but I am not taking you on my team. We have our guys already."

I felt a heaviness in my chest like I was on an operating table, and they were giving me compressions. Somehow, I managed to calmly thank him for the opportunity, shook his hand, looked him in the eyes, and told him I would succeed. I think this response just came naturally to me because of the manners instilled in me by my grandmother, but this also wasn't my first rejection. My next move had to be to accept it and move on. There was no time to feel bad for myself because I had to make a decision. This door was now officially closed. The question was what should I do now?

Walking out of the field house, I met up with my buddy, Jon, who had seen the tryouts. He was shocked to learn the outcome of the tryout because he thought I had an amazing go at it. He may have also likened me to Michael Jordan.

"Come on. Was I that good?"

"Yeah, you looked great out there. You were playing real, competitive basketball."

Jon was an important friend to me during this time. My financial aid didn't cover a dorm room for the school year. He was letting me sleep on his floor. I appreciated him letting me shower and crash there. We spent many nights eating a late-night snack at the café or shooting baskets. When he told me I had played well at the tryout, I trusted his opinion.

One night, I went for a walk alone around the campus. I used the time to think about what I was going to do after the semester, and it hit me: Western Connecticut State University was still an option. I called the coach and said, "Hi, Coach. This is Shawn Mobilio. I want to play basketball for you. It's not working out here at SCSU."

"We would love to have you, Shawn," he said. "Apply for a transfer, and we will start by having you play pickup with the guys at open runs."

It wasn't meant for me to be at Southern Connecticut State University, so I finished my semester and was accepted to WCSU. Sometimes, you need failure to succeed. Life is about how you handle any situation that comes at you. I will never forget all the teachable moments I had and how those former and new coaches made me feel. My vow was to make sure when I coach one day to always be honest and care for each of my players. Failure and fear hold people back. Imagine if there was no failure in life. How would we learn? How would we get ahead in life? Adversity brings out the true character in an individual. My journey was not even close to the finish line. I still needed to work hard to transfer and play for my new school.

Chapter 10

Riding the Pine

I was told the arena had a beautiful new floor. The only time I had seen it was on my brief

tour of the campus back during my senior year of high school. Now as the ball hit the hardwood,

it bounced nicely back into my hand. "This will do," I thought to myself with a broad smile.

Coach had called me in for a first meeting, and as I was shooting around to burn off my nervous

energy. Players and coaches were watching from above in the film room. I didn't know how to

get up there, so I stayed right where I was, putting on a show. Eventually, a player was sent down

to get me. We walked up a few flights of stairs and down a hallway to the film room. The team

was gathered in the middle, watching a conference competitor we would be playing in two weeks

I shook all the coach's hands and quietly walked to the back to sit down. The players were

skeptically looking at me.

"This is Shawn Mobilio. He is a transfer from SCSU and is a new member of this team.

Please make him feel welcome," the coach said when he introduced me to the room.

One of the assistants yelled out, "He's not that good. Don't worry." His wink at me told me

he was obviously kidding around.

Another assistant coach was dissecting the game and designing plays. I was impressed with

his craft. And as the film continued, he was explaining things that I hadn't noticed on my own. It

was one of the first times I saw a basketball game as a strategy rather than talent and skill.

After the film was over, we went downstairs to practice. The assistant coach grabbed me and

said, "Hope you were paying attention. Most these guys have been here for a few years." He let me know the coach had a winning record with over five hundred wins. Good players were recruited, some from other college teams, and this year the team was ranked in the country for Division III. Most schools in this division are satisfied with just being ranked because it is considered an accomplishment. However, WCSU wanted to win a national championship. The players who transferred from Division I or II to play Division III did so for the sole purpose of getting more playing time. They would also have a better chance of winning a national championship.

We warmed up and formed a five-man weave going three-on-two back. This was an intense first practice. I could see why this team was ranked. My team. I wasn't used to being on a team anymore, and it felt great to say, "My team." The starting point guard/shooting guard was the fastest guy I ever played against on the court. His handle was amazing, his shot was amazing, and his IQ for the game was exceptional. This was the kind of player I wanted to guard every day in practice. I could make him better, and he could make me better.

Another new experience was using a punch code to get into the locker room. I immediately forgot it and had to ask how to get in. I didn't see the point guard in the hallway, so I walked back into the gym. He was there, getting up more shots. I watched as he made shot after shot with his left hand. It's rare to see a left-handed shooter, and he was certainly a "lefty lights out shooter." I put my shoes right back on, and I started shooting on the other side. An hour went by, and he walked back to the locker room. I stayed and shot a few more before going back in. He heard me knock, opened the door, and went back to sitting in the corner of the locker room on his phone.

"Hi," I said to him. He nodded his head. "Guess he's not much of a talker," I thought to myself.

When I was walking out, one of the players, tall with long hair, looked familiar to me. As I approached, I realized it was Gary Robinson, a guy I played against in high school. He immediately noticed me, and we hit it off. He invited me to his room to show me some recorded plays. Gary was a big and tall guy. I was surprised he was so friendly, and I suppose had he been a guard, he wouldn't have been. Later, he became one of my best friends on the team and was a great resource.

At practice, we started to drill offense, and I was on the second team, running the point guard. I played the starting point guard hard; his moves were effective until I started to use my body. Using my strength and weight to my advantage was key, so when I bumped him, he would lose balance and sometimes lose control of the ball. He would also lose control of his emotions. It was clear he didn't appreciate my physical game, but I didn't care—I wanted to take that spot. He was good, and he knew it. The coaches let him do whatever he wanted, probably because he was a senior, averaging twenty points. They loved him, but he didn't respect the coaches.

The first game arrived in no time. Dan let me know he was watching it live on the internet. He sent me a note that I kept in my locker that said,

Shawn,

You've been cut, you've been knocked down, coaches let you go, but you never gave up. You believed when no one else did. That's why you are where you are today. Keep going, no matter how hard it gets! All heart!

I kissed that note, folded it, and thanked God for giving me my family and friends.

Not only was it the first game of the season, it was my first college game. I hadn't attended a game here before, so I wasn't sure what to expect. We entered to music blasting in the huge arena. The fans were pumped. As I ran to the warm-up lines, I looked around and saw my rothers in the bleachers. What an amazing feeling to hear the fans screaming and to see my amily. It was showtime!

The starting lineup was announced, and I wasn't in it. The point guard was having a great ame in the first half. He already had eighteen points. Gary played awesome, as well. But I didn't ven get off the bench. I looked back at my brothers, and I knew they felt for me. During the alftime speech, the coach was talking, but my mind was scrambled. I didn't even know what vas going on because I was clouded with anger. I just wanted to play. But I wasn't put in during ne second half either.

The final horn went off, and we had won. While shaking hands with the other team, I had ears in my eyes. I said goodbye to my brothers and thanked them for coming. In the locker room, veryone was happy but me. This wasn't how I wanted my first college game to go. I sat in front f my locker, head down, until everyone left. I still had to shower. Gary gave me a sympathetic ook and said, "Keep your head up, kid."

A custodian walked in to sweep the floor. Tears were running down my cheeks, and he asked f I was okay. I kind of lost it. "No, man. I can't catch a damn break. Everywhere I go, I have to ight to do what I love. Why can't people see I'm giving one hundred percent and play me?"

He laughed and said, "Bro, you're kind of short."

"Doesn't matter. I have the biggest heart you will ever see on this court."

"Then keep working. If you are good, you will get in."

I grabbed my towel and took a shower. While the water was dripping on my head, I prayed nd told God that I was not quitting. Somehow, I was going to work harder. If you really want omething in life, you have to get it.

I was commuting back and forth to school from Seymour, so this made my life a bit complicated. Instead of driving home at night, I slept in the film room. No one knew. I would watch film for a few hours and fall asleep. My alarm rang every morning at 5:00 a.m. The workers came in by 5:30, so I had enough time to get to the court before they arrived. After my practice session, I went to breakfast, class, took time to study, and then went to practice. Finally, climbed the stairs to watch more film and sleep right there in the room. I didn't have much money for gas and without a job, I was living off my small income tax refund check. It covered my food and gas some months. I continued to do this for the whole year without being discovered.

Another complication was that I switched majors from physical education to communications. I had some additional courses I needed to take in order to stay on track for graduation in two years.

Eventually, Coach put me in for a few minutes each game, and I finally scored my first college points. A few refs asked me why I wasn't playing more. I didn't know what to say. One game, I had ten points and four assists despite playing only fourteen minutes. If I went in for the starting point guard, he would go back to the bench and complain that I was in for him. I wasn't impressed with his team spirit. He was projected to be an All-American that year. It was funny to see him get all mad, especially when I had a good game or when I was competing with him in practice. We battled every day. I thought we were making each other better. Apparently, he didn' agree.

One of our big games was against Keene State College. Their team's point guard was a Division I transfer. He was a small, quick guard who could play, but our starting guard was much better. The game was tied halfway through the first half. Our starting guard was having a bad game. Coach looked down the bench and said, "Shawn, let's go. You're in!" I sprinted over to the score table while an assistant coach yelled at me to stick with that guard. Bringing the ball up, the

uard was on me but was giving me a little room. Eventually I was deep, around the NBA three-
oint line. I let it go. Nothing but net! The fans were going crazy, and I was so happy Joe was
1ere to see that moment.

"Steal by Mobilio" the announcer said. I pulled up for two points and hit the shot. I was
eginning to get in a zone where I couldn't be stopped. This was the moment I was waiting for
1y whole life, and it was my time to unleash the beast within. I faked like I was setting a set
creen and pulled from three-point range again. It went right in! Joe was now running up and
own the sidelines. He was proud of his younger brother, and I was pumped that he was there.
Ve ended up winning the game. I had eighteen points and six assists against a team that was also
anked in our division. Walking off the court, everyone now knew who I was. The energy from
1e crowd was electric. I hugged my brother and walked into the locker room. My teammates
ame up to me and showed me a lot of love. I was the last one in the locker room, and my
leaning crew buddy came by to sweep.

"Can I tell you something, Shawn?"

"Sure," I said.

"That was amazing. You have what it takes. Keep working, kid."

I thanked him and went in to shower. While my head was down, I said to myself, "My dream
as been hit with dirt since I started, but I kept shaking it off, and I kept moving." Most people
eal with life not wanting to feel pain and disappointment. With no pain, there is no gain. When I
vent to sleep that night in the film room, it was the first night of my life I think I actually slept a
ull night of good sleep.

The word courage comes from Anglo-French origin meaning "from heart." In life, you are going to go through hard times and that's okay. Courage is not about medals, awards, or prizes. It's really about what you feel is right in your heart.

The starting point guard went on to play on the All-American team. I truly believe that if we never played against each other, he wouldn't have received that award. On the other hand, I would have never gotten to where I am. We pushed each other every day. Most college players will go through their career playing and just getting by. Not us. We both learned from each other and he made me a better player. Not many people can say that; not many can sit behind an All-American and not quit. I am grateful for the competitiveness we shared. If you asked him today about the toughest player he played against, he would say it was me.

Chapter 11

Doubt Me Now

The sound of keys jingling and the door shaking woke me up. Just as my eyes opened, a police officer came in. "What are you doing here?" I began to stutter and could barely apologize for being there. He listened to my explanation about watching game film and falling asleep. Then he asked, "Are you that little point guard for the school?" I told him I was. We engaged in a conversation where he complimented me and talked about my senior year. He wished me luck and walked out. I thought for sure I was in trouble and let out a huge sigh of relief when I realized he was cool with me.

The coach named me the starting point guard for my last year of college basketball. All the pieces were coming together for me, or so I thought. There were forty players that tried out for the team, and only fifteen made it. A few new players transferred in. The first few games were good, but we were having a tough year as a team. We didn't have a good groove going to make things happen. Coach was starting me sometimes, but not all of the time. It began to bother me mentally, and I struggled to stay focused. I had a special bond with Coach Ken, one of the assistants. At times, he reminded me of Dan because of his support and encouragement. Coach Ken was instrumental in helping me through this challenging time.

After a late practice, I received a phone call from my brother. He informed me Coach Josh, our coach from our childhood, had died suddenly. Sadly, I had lost touch with Josh over the past few years. Reflecting on all that he meant to me as my first real coach and mentor, I realized he had been one of my best coaches. I was where I was because of his support, his love, and his belief in me. His death broke my heart, but I didn't tell anyone on the team or my coaches. I didn't want them to feel bad or make excuses for me. This was my first experience losing someone really close. He taught me the game. Coach Josh helped the youth in Naugatuck, and he will never be forgotten.

The day after I heard the news, we had a game. I was off and couldn't hit a shot, so the coach moved in another recruit to the starting point guard position. I felt knocked down again.

I heard a whisper in my ear. "Are you going to give up?" I broke down and cried. The voice sounded just like Josh. He was speaking to me as my angel, telling me I came too far to give up. The message came just as I was right on the edge of quitting the team.

We are all human and when death happens, it's not easy to get over. Time allowed me to get out of my funk. Classes were going well. I was starting to think about my life after college. Perhaps I should try to play basketball in Europe. But for now, my main focus was on finishing the season strong. There was a big game coming up against a team from Boston. I was not in the starting lineup, but I was determined to dominate in that game, and that's exactly what I did. We won, and my stats included eighteen points, nine assists, eight rebounds, and five steals. Dan texted me, congratulating me on such a great game. I was back to playing the game with confidence and feeling like myself. The team named me co-captain, and I finished the regular season third in the Little East Conference for assists.

Despite our struggles, our team made the playoffs. The first round had us facing Eastern Connecticut State University. If we didn't win, this would be the last game for the seniors. We traveled to play in their gym. Not surprisingly, the place was packed with a lot of enthusiastic fans. I was in the training room getting my ankles taped as the Eastern players came walking in. My head phones were on, and I didn't pay too much attention to them. It was more important to focus on being competitive when it was game time.

Our pregame talk took place upstairs in a classroom. This is where the coach went over the starting line-up and the game plan. The board didn't include my name. That broke me down—it really did. What kind of game was the coach playing? I had had enough. This could be my very last college game, and I wasn't starting. The whole time he was going over the starting line-up, I sat there with a look of disgust on my face. We were in the league playoffs, and I'd been fighting for two years to be a starter.

I only played twenty minutes the whole game. The fire was just not there for me to put in tremendous effort to win for this coach. Sometimes a player can only take so much. We went on to lose by fourteen points, and my college career was over. Just like that. After the game, he dismissed the seniors from the after-game talk so he could address the underclassmen privately. All the seniors commiserated and hugged one another before getting on the bus quietly. It was a rough year for the team, and it was frustrating for the coaches, as well.

Sitting in the back of the bus, the hood of my sweatshirt covered my face. I was upset not only with the coach but with myself. A bad attitude affected my game because I let it. When we stopped for dinner, most of the seniors didn't get off to eat. The underclassmen bought their food and came back on the bus. One of the players approached me. "Did you hear he was talking about you?" Apparently, the coach told the team that I had a dream to play basketball overseas. His opinion was that I was too short and would never play in that arena. Furthermore, no one else should get their hopes up either. Unbelievable. His negative attitude was now being spread to the entire team, and he was using me as an example for failure. I was grateful to receive this information. It was exactly what I needed to hear at the right time. This was the motivation I needed. My next step would be to play overseas. My career wasn't over yet.

PART 4

LIFE AFTER COLLEGE

Chapter 12

Refocus

I was the first member of my family to graduate college. I was excited and proud of myself! My family was also proud of me. I had worked hard, and this was a huge accomplishment. Joe had opted to work for my dad's family business, and Mike was attending SCSU. Neither of them continued to play basketball after high school. It didn't matter. The Mobilio brothers were now men, individually working toward our own goals, supporting one another the best we could. We were all still living with our father in Seymour, and we would see our mother and her side of the family on the weekends.

Once I decided that I wanted to play basketball overseas, I kicked back into training mode. It felt natural to work toward a goal. Over the summer, a friend of mine called and asked if we could practice together. He had been a professional basketball player in Italy for a few years. At one of our sessions, he asked me if I was going to an international tryout in North Carolina. The USA Select Team that toured all over Europe was trying to find jobs for guys who wanted to play professionally. I hadn't heard of the program, so I did some research. I also called the general manager, Sean Kilmartin.

"Hi! My name is Shawn Mobilio. I'm from Connecticut, and I want to try out for your team

"How tall are you? What college did you attend?"

"I'm five feet, eight inches, and Western Connecticut State University."

"Sorry, man, you won't stand a chance." Then he hung up.

This wasn't my first rodeo, so I called him right back.

"I need to know where this tryout is taking place. Tell me the location, time, and a hotel you
recommend."

"These are Division II and top Division I guys."

"Yup, and I'm ready to compete. At my tryout, you'll see."

He laughed and gave me all the information. I wondered how often he hung up on other
players. Did they call back like me? No matter what he thought, my dream was to play overseas,
and I would get my shot.

The tryout would consist of three days of games, five games per day. This meant I needed to
be in the best shape of my life. Fifteen games over three days would require incredible stamina,
focus, and strength. For two months, I trained harder than I ever had before. A new technique I
added was to video record my training so I could critique myself. All those nights watching film
at WCSU provided the inspiration for this addition. Most of my sessions were twice a day, lasting
four hours each time. Eating and hydrating was a big priority. My family thought I was crazy, but
this was something I had to do. I also obtained a passport so I would ready to go when chosen.

I flew to Charlotte, North Carolina for the tryouts. This was my first time traveling alone.
Funds were tight, so I rented the cheapest car I could afford. It had no power steering, and I had
to use my muscles on every turn. While unpacking at the hotel, I put the local TV news on. Sean

Kilmartin, the general manager of the USA Select Team, was talking about the camp and how it is used to help players have an opportunity to be seen and to sign guys on overseas teams. I thought that was pretty cool to see this guy on television, and here I was trying out for his team. If he was a star, I was going to be star too.

An inspirational tool I used was to create sticky notes with motivational quotes so I could hang them on my mirror, near my bed, and on the door. I brought them with me, and I hung them around my hotel room. I believe if you attract positive, you will receive positive. Dinner was a peanut butter and jelly sandwich I brought with me from home. As I pulled out the plastic bag, it was a little warm and a little squished, but that was my dinner that night. Even though I had little money, I would have to stop at the store and get sports drinks, water, and some food for the next few days. Money was tight, but at least I had a bed to sleep in.

The next morning, I was up at 5:00 a.m. to stretch. I reread my sticky notes:

You got this

Never give up

You never get tired

The continental breakfast in the hotel had a nice selection, especially because it was "all you can eat." I had five hard boiled eggs, fruit, and yogurt. A few extra yogurts and fruit might have made it back to the fridge in my room to snack on later.

The check-in for tryouts was in the same hotel where I was staying. I went strolling down the staircase and approached the booth. While waiting in line, I was sizing up my competition—they were huge. They must have been eating way more than peanut butter and jelly. Most of these guys were from the United States, but some were from around the world. I wondered how many f them had to work as hard as I did to earn their place on a team. How many were given ositions purely because of their size?

Everyone that worked for the USA Select Team organization was welcoming. A muscular, all man with slicked back hair approached me. "Hi! I'm Sean."

I replied, "I'm Shawn."

"From Connecticut?" I knew at once he was chuckling about the fact I had lied about my eight. Good! He remembered me. My height increased just a bit when he gave me a jersey and horts and told me to be at the courts by 3:00 p.m. sharp.

"Yes, sir," I answered.

Chapter 13

The Tryout

Athletes are prone to injuries because of the quick and awkward movements we often make. Athletic tape is a must. It provides the necessary support to keep joints in line. You also have to make sure you put some type of support on both heels so you don't get irritation and blisters. I had to learn to tape my own ankles when I wasn't on a team. There wasn't an athletic trainer to do it for me, so I had to do it. It is painful without support. I learned a trick when taping your own ankles. I used a paper towel and folded it into a square as I held it against my heel. Then I began to tape right on to it. By using tape without pre-wrap, it felt more secure. After watching trainers and videos, I became a pro. I also learned I had to shave my legs. Once, I tried it without shaving and it was like waxing my legs. It hurt, and I screamed. After both ankles are taped, I put on two pairs of socks: one low ankle sock and one high sock. It's something I'd done since high school. Laundry day consisted of lots of socks!

Before leaving my hotel room, I glanced over at all my motivating notes. I was nervous. On my way to the gym, I said to myself, "If this is meant to be, it will happen. All I need to do is work hard and enjoy the game of basketball, just like Coach Josh taught me." The facility at Carolina Courts had six full courts with coaches all over the place looking for talent to take on this international trip to Europe. There were over four hundred players sitting on the bleachers, waiting to try out. I knew only thirty-eight players would be chosen. That was less than ten percent! Most of the players were tall and bulky. I was fairly certain I was the smallest and the only Division III player there. We all had the same goal. This was war, and I was pleased I had worked so hard to be in the best shape possible.

Sean introduced himself and his coaching staff. We had five games each day for three days; fifteen games in a short amount of time. After breaking up into teams, we stretched with a military guy. He also reminded me of my buddy Marcello from my boxing days. I enjoyed it because he made everyone count out loud. This brought a lot of energy to the gym and to me as well.

My first game was successful because I pushed the ball every play, knowing I could outwork most of these guys. As the point guard, I passed the ball to the open guy, and when I had a shot or an open lane, I fearlessly took it. Sean called me over after my team won and sat me down.

"Shawn, do you have your passport?"

"Yes, it's with me in my bag. Are we going now?"

He laughed. "No, but I love your game and would like to know if you would be interested in traveling with us in September."

I jumped up and answered, "Yes!"

"Keep working hard. We have our eyes on you."

After day one, I was walking out of the gym, and one of the coaches approached me. "Being in the shape that you are shows you are taking this seriously. You're the one guy who is in the best shape here." I thanked him for the compliment. From that moment on, I had the confidence I needed. My hard work was finally paying off.

I was a little sore but feeling good. Some guys didn't play in all of the games because they were either dehydrated or cramped up. This showed the coaches they were not in shape or not playing smart, which most likely meant they didn't stand a chance. Some guys just left and went home. This made it easier for the coaches to decide who would be chosen for the team. While heading back to the hotel, I hydrated. Food was provided at the tryout, so I brought some back to my room. I planned to go to bed early to be ready for the second day. It was 10:00 p.m., and I heard lots of noises coming from the hallway. When I opened my door, a player that recognized me said, "Hey, J. J. Barea. You want to come to the club with us?" I laughed at his comparison o me to the NBA player who is about five feet eight inches tall. Most of these guys didn't understand the opportunity that was right in front of them. I did, so I declined the invitation and went to bed.

Day two was going to be long, so I made sure to have a good breakfast. Heading over to the gym, I was several hours early. It gave me time to stretch and warm-up. The gym was empty— just the way I loved it. By 10:00 a.m., everyone was ready to start. There was a significant drop i the number of players, and it would only get worse throughout the day. My plan was to continue pushing the ball, showing the coaches I can run, and moving the ball. European basketball is quick, and I wanted to prove to them that I could run an offense. It wasn't about scoring forty points or more. All I had to do was find the open guy and get the ball down the court. When I wa open, I scored, but finding open guys was going to get me noticed more. As predicted, guys continued to drop like flies. Injuries set in and if you were not in shape, it was easy to get hurt an pull muscles. My team dropped to only seven guys. As point guard, I had to hold everyone together and tell them, "It's just us, but we can do this." I was happy to demonstrate my leadership abilities.

My team made it to the finals, to be held on the third day, and all eyes were on us. During th championship game, we ran out of gas, and I was tired as well. Sean walked up to me and said, "You need to work more on that left hand." I thought my left hand was pretty good, but I thanke him for the suggestion.

Before we left, the coaches met with each of the teams. Names were being called. "Shawn Mobilio...red team." My name was called! I was on a team! I headed over to the back room where other guys on the red team sat. Congratulating us all, Sean told us he had information on where we were going. We would be traveling all over the United Kingdom for a month. He told us we needed passports and that we needed to pay a fee. This fee included games, practices, airfare, train pass, and hotel. Everything else was on us. The fee was $3,500, plus the additional expenses. My heart almost dropped. We all looked at each other. We have to pay to go on this trip? None of us seemed to know this.

"You will receive an email with all the information. We leave for training camp in September. Congrats! See you all soon."

We collectively left there thinking, "How are we going to come up with this money?" Most college graduates have student loans and debt. We just paid to come to this tryout. Now this. We would have to pay to play.

I needed a plan. If you really want something, you have to make it happen. I sat in my rental car, hands on the steering wheel jerking back and forth while I cried happy tears. I was so excited that I made the team. YES, I MADE IT! I called everyone and told them the good news. My team was really happening. Now all I needed to do was figure out how to come up with the money to travel overseas.

Chapter 14

Mobilio Dream fundraiser

As the water filled up the tub in the hotel room, I limped over to shut it off before it overflowed. I had a few hours before I needed to pack up and head over to the airport, so I decided to take an ice bath. This is the craziest thing an athlete can do, but it's the best trick in the book. After working incredibly hard for a prolonged period of time, the body cramps up, especially lower extremities. An ice bath helps the muscles recover faster. It helps every time. You can't just inch in slowly—that doesn't work. You need to dive right in. After throwing the ice in, I held my breath and took the plunge. The first ten minutes were like torture. I tried to stay still so it didn't hurt as much. After I acclimated, my muscles began to loosen.

I packed my bags and headed to the airport with my body feeling amazing. My plan was to figure out what comes next, so I put a pen and notebook in my carry-on bag. I had the window seat, which wouldn't be bad depending on who I sat next to. On my flight to North Carolina, I sat next to someone who was coughing and sneezing the whole time. At first, I convinced myself that he would stop. I thought to myself, "Maybe he has a little tickle in the throat." Twenty minutes, later it got worse. I put on my headphones and watched whatever movie was playing on the plane. Now that I was taking my seat to fly home, I chuckled as I remembered this experience. It hit me that he had been reading a book about fundraising. I had an idea right then and there. Maybe I could fundraise to make my dream possible! The brainstorming began, and I wrote down any idea that came to me.

• Ask business owners to sponsor me

• Order T-shirts and put their business logos on the back

•Pledge to wear the shirt while I toured Europe

•Sell the shirts to people to raise additional money and for businesses to get their logos
seen

This was going to work, I told myself.

When I arrived, the first thing my dad said was, "What do you mean you have to pay to go on
his trip to play basketball?"

"Nice to see you too, Dad. Yes, I need to come up with $3,500 in order for me to play."

"I think it's time for you to get a job and forget about this basketball crap."

To clear my head from this disappointing welcome home, I went to the basketball court in the
earby park to put up a quick five hundred jump shots. My father just didn't understand. He was
ever an athlete. His life was modeled around getting a job with benefits and saving your money.
ut that's not what I wanted. It was important to me to be happy with what I was doing. Money
as just a tool; it didn't create happiness. Dad hated that I didn't have a job and that I was living
nder his roof. It didn't matter that I had a chance to make my dream come true.

My dad's brother and sister-in-law were a great resource. They helped me understand what I
eeded to do. My uncle took care of the administrative business side of the family business, so he
ally understood finances and salesmanship. He and my aunt suggested I create a non-profit

organization. They were the brains behind this proposal and provided the information I needed to follow through with it.

To make money for the extra expenses, I worked as a certified personal trainer during the day at a corporate gym in our community. After work, I visited local businesses to solicit sponsorship. Asking for money made me feel like a salesman. I had a folder of information to distribute, and I explained my story. Many doors slammed in my face, and companies flat out rejected me. When did that ever stop me? Eventually, I had ten businesses committed. My dad was upset because he felt I shouldn't be asking people for money. It didn't matter to him that the sponsorship was reciprocal. The donations I received provided the resources I needed to design and create the T-shirts. On the front was USA SELECT and the number 14. The back included my last name and the ten sponsors. In addition to the shirts, I created a page on social media, visited schools, and talked to youth teams. I was determined to sell lots of shirts. The local papers interviewed me and printed articles, which helped spread the word quickly. I sold just over one hundred shirts to amazing, generous people. Some didn't even know me but still wanted to help. The end result was that I raised over $4,000 in just one month. This meant I had additional funds for food while I was on the tour. I am still grateful for all the sponsors, family, and friends who believed in me.

The head coach at Western Connecticut State University was wrong about me. It would have been nice to see his reaction every time he logged into his WCSU account and saw the article that said, "Athlete gets an 'assist' from his degree as he pursues his dream." The headline captured it all. I was blessed that he told me I wouldn't make it. His statement drove me to where I was, and I was thankful—not mad.

With the money raised, I spent the final two weeks working hard to improve my game. Sean's comment about my left-hand usage was bouncing around in my brain. I started using my left hand for everything. I opened doors with my left hand, ate and drank left-handed, dribbled and shot with my left hand, and I even wrote left-handed. Training camp would be yet another opportunity for me to make a statement. You need to make your weaknesses your strengths, and that's exactly what I did. Soon I would be on my way to travel the world and live my dreams playing in Ireland, Scotland, London, and Whales.

I was getting ready to leave, and all my family, friends, and sponsors where there to say goodbye. It was touching and will always be a gratifying memory. I could feel their love and support, and it was the last bit of energy I needed before going on this next journey. Driving to the airport with my mom, Joe, Joe's baby son, and Mike, all I could think about was how much love we had for each other. Outside the terminal, my brothers and I went in for one more huddle like the Team Image days. We actually put our hands in and said, "On three…Mobilio brothers!" I know Coach Josh was looking down, smiling from heaven, while my brothers were right there watching me go for my dreams.

I boarded the plane to return to North Carolina for training camp. This was a short flight compared to the eight-and-a-half-hour flight to London. How would I sit still for that long? After landing in Charlotte, there was a bus waiting to take us to the prep school that would host our training camp. The bus was packed by the time my flight came in, and I didn't have a seat. One of the coaches, a tall Greek man who played professional basketball in Greece, was there and saw me standing around. He introduced himself as Nick and told me I could ride with him. I was thrilled to sit up front in his Porsche SUV for the hour-long ride. He asked me about my story, so I told him about my college experiences and how I ended up at the training camp.

"Your father must be so proud of you," he suggested.

"He really doesn't like the fact that I'm doing this, and he doesn't want to financially support me. So, I raised the money on my own."

He looked over at me and said, "You know, Shawn, I had the same problem with my father. He cut hair and wanted me to do the same. He actually cut Elvis Presley's hair once and wanted me to take over the business. I did the same thing you are doing, and I ended up playing professional basketball in Greece."

"Yeah, that's the same for my dad. He wants me to work for him so my brothers and I can take over his business."

"One day, you and your father will laugh about this, and he will be so proud of you like my father is now."

What were the chances we would have the same kind of father? This was so strange to me, but it was comforting to relate to him. Nick told me to keep doing what I was doing, and he was proud of me. How amazing that I just met this man not even an hour ago, yet we became quick friends. It felt like more angels were coming my way.

Chapter 15

Training Camp

When we arrived at the prep school, I helped Nick bring in some food. I was starving and couldn't wait to eat. There where ten rooms reserved for us with bunk beds. That turned out to be not enough. All the rooms and beds were spoken for before I arrived. One of the coaches told me I would need to sleep in the common living room area with three other players. They were pissed off and whining, but I didn't really care because I was used to sleeping on the floor. Plus, I was just excited for training camp to start. It was this experience of not having a room that allowed the four of us to become good friends over the next three days. We tried to make it fun and that made us closer. Most of the other guys didn't even talk to each other. They were either on their phones with their girlfriends or had their headphones on. I had a cell phone with me to call home, but that was not something I did often.

I didn't have anywhere to hang my motivational cards, so I kept them in my bag. Before leaving for practice each day, I made sure to read them. This was an important part of my morning routine to make sure I had the encouragement I needed to do my best.

All the players at the training camp had one goal—to be picked up by a professional team. Everyone was ready to commit and earn their spot. On the first night, I found an old chapel on campus where I could pray before curfew. My grandmother made me promise to pray each night while I was away. A promise is a promise, and I went into the dark and gloomy building, but I felt safe. As a young boy, I would walk into church and pray about being the best basketball player I could be. Walking in this time, I prayed the same thing, but I also prayed for my family and friends, and for the coaches and the players here. I knew I would be okay no matter what happened. I felt mature. Life is short, and you need to enjoy it no matter what is thrown at you.

Alarms went off in the bunks. The coaches were running through the hallways, banging on doors, and blowing their whistles to wake everyone up. Guys were rolling around, slow to get up for the first full day of training camp. I was already up and eating breakfast in the kitchen. A teammate came walking in. He was a six-foot-five shooting guard from a Division I school in Iowa.

"Good morning! Nice to be up early, huh?" I greeted him.

"I'm always up."

I laughed because this was the only basketball player I had met with the same drive to be first in the morning. He and I were both at the gym early—the first ones there. I learned my new pal, Bobby, also liked to get some shots up after form shooting and free throws. We were in a full sweat by the time everyone showed up twenty minutes later.

After team warmups, we did a lot of running, both on the court and learning plays. Most of the guys ran off the court after practice to get back to bed or to eat. Bobby was walking off the court too, so I yelled over to him. With a sly smile, he wiped the sweat off his face and ran over to get some shots up. Two hours later, we were the only ones still in the gym. We pushed each other. Shooting after we were tired not only helped us physically but mentally as well.

The custodian was amused as he watched from the top of the bleachers, and he approached us after our workout. He told us a story about when he was a player and played overseas for a year before blowing out his knee.

"Playing this game, you have to understand it won't last forever. Your body can only take so much. You have to cherish the moments you have now."

This was a powerful statement, and it stuck with me. Walking back to my makeshift room, I thought, "He's right. I have to figure out what I will do after basketball is over." Most players don't think this way because they dream of making millions and being set for life. Planning for a future with no basketball is not usually part of the equation. That night, I thought about this, but I also wanted to enjoy what I was doing in the moment.

During the time I was at the prep school, I liked going to the chapel when no one was in there. Most days, I went after lunch. Praying helped me a lot—it kept me grounded. I wasn't really feeling homesick because training and the trip to Europe distracted me enough. But praying offered a connection to home. One day as I was walking out, I saw a man toward the corner, kneeling in the back row. It was the custodian who had given me great advice. He called me over, and I sat down with him. We chatted about how much he missed playing and coaching.

"Where did you coach?" I asked him.

He replied, "I coached college and helped out with the Charlotte Bobcats for a while."

"The professional team?"

"Yes," he answered.

"What happened? Why aren't you still doing that?"

"It was a lot of traveling. I was getting older, and my wife passed away."

My emotions immediately kicked in. "I'm sorry."

"She's in Heaven now." His belief in God kept him going, and I thought this was remarkable. He told me he arrived at work every day at 6:00 a.m.

"Is it okay if I came in to shoot around?"

"You remind me of myself as a kid. Keep working hard, and you'll find where you belong."

Walking out of the church, I felt sorry for the man. He was alone in this world, working until he meets his wife again. It felt right to honor his advice, so I grabbed my gear to head back to the gym to get some shots up. Like most successful people, you have to perfect your craft. I basically lived in the gym and on the court for my entire basketball career. To most college and professional coaches, this is the type of player they love to bring into their program. You can have all the talent in the world, but if you don't work at it, then you will be outworked by someone else.

Night practice started, and it consisted of a lot of stretching before multiple games. I'd gone through pre-practice rituals before, but this was the first time stretching before a workout was treated this seriously. I appreciated the concern for our bodies and well-being. We ran through our plays, going full court. Coach brought us in and told us to get right to sleep so we would be ready for the next day. Everyone grabbed their stuff and headed toward the bunks. I was getting my towel, and I was beat. From across the court, I heard my voice. This time it was Bobby encouraging me to stay and practice more. Walking over to him, I was satisfied that this guy was going to push me, and I was going to push him. After five hundred shots were made, the lights went off. There was no way for us to see where our bags were. Both of us tried to find our cell

hones to use as flashlights. I heard a loud thump, like a body falling. Poor Bobby went down
ard because he fell over a chair. I thought he might be hurt, but he began to laugh.

"Stop being so clumsy, dude!" I chided him.

"You're short! You don't have this problem." We both laughed.

It was a rough night because most of the guys stayed up late. I was used to going to bed early.
here was little privacy in my makeshift room, so I was feeling frustrated. Still, I fell asleep.

I woke up at 5:30 a.m. to have breakfast. Practice started again at 7:00. I figured I could eat
nd be on the court by 6:00. Bobby and I agreed to meet to get shots up. Walking to the court, I
ok in the cool air and birds chirping. It helped me feel ready for the day. At 5:52 a.m., my
ustodian friend pulled up.

"Good morning," he called over.

I replied, "You're late, sir."

"You're a crazy kid," he laughed.

I ran into the gym, smelling the familiar scent of a wood court. It was nice to be the first one
again. By 6:30, there was no sign of Bobby. I gave it a bit of thought, guessing he must be
ally tired. In life, there are people who kind of want it and then there are people who want it! At
:45, Sean walked in and noted that I was the first one there. I think he sounded proud.

Practice went well. We were understanding the plays and working as a team. It was nice to be
n a court where everyone had a great IQ for the game and understood that it's a team sport. In
rder to get picked up by a professional organization overseas, you need to have court smarts, not
st talent. I was learning from my mistakes in college. My attitude was improving.

Bobby was having a bad shooting day and when practice was over, I walked over to him. "Let's put up some shots."

"I'm not in the mood today," he complained.

"What's up?"

"My shot's off."

I thought joking with him would snap him out of it. "Stop sleeping in then!" But he didn't laugh. Clearly, he needed some teammate support from me, so I told him, "Listen, man, we are human. We are all going to have bad days. That's okay. We live to fight another day, man." He began to walk away, and I said, "Come on, let's shoot." He reluctantly walked back and got shot up with me.

Leaving the court, I saw the custodian looking at me. "You have a gift to motivate people," he told me.

"God gave me this gift."

"You are absolutely right, kid."

My relationship with this custodian was special. I don't know what it was, but I felt naturally close to the custodians at every school I attended. They ran the schools, and I was always there to practice. Perhaps just seeing each other every day helped to form strong bonds. I asked this gentleman to shoot with me, and he came onto the court. Here was this seventy-year-old man shooting the ball with a huge smile on his face. I will never forget that moment. Basketball doesn't just teach you about the game—it teaches you about life.

The last day of training camp didn't have much running. The coaches gave us the itinerary and went through the rules. Everything was planned out very well, and I was impressed. New jerseys and shorts were distributed. After the session, we washed our clothes in the laundry room. It was important that we all left with clean clothes because there were no laundry rooms in the hotels where we would be staying. We would have to find a laundromat or use the bathroom sink and air dry our clothes. That was something I knew how to do.

Travel to London was early the next day. Because of the time change, we had to be ready for the jetlag. That night, the management team brought us to an Italian restaurant where they had a big buffet table. Only some of the coaches joined us because not all would travel with us. We ate like kings. They thanked us and wished us lots of success. The team was separated by level of competition. Sean placed me on the high-end team with more skills and talent. Before going to bed, I strolled down to the chapel one last time. The custodian was there in the corner he preferred for quiet prayer time.

"This is it, huh?" he asked.

"Yes, on our way to London tomorrow."

"I've been watching you play during practice. I like your style. You're a tough guard, like Mighty Mouse." We both laughed at the reference. "You keep playing hard and keep being the point guard. I see you being famous one day."

I thanked him and said, "I have a long way to go, sir."

"You aren't too far away. Believe me. Not many people have the opportunity to do what you are doing, especially at your height."

I agreed with him. "But my heart overpowers my height." We shook hands before I left.

When I headed back to the bunks, I ran into Sean and told him what a nice guy that custodian was. He looked confused. He told me there were no custodians on campus while we were there, only campus police. I told him I must have been mistaken but really, I was in shock. Who was that man I'd been speaking to? An angel sent from above? Was I seeing things? Was I dehydrated? Bobby had been with me the first time I met him, so he must be real. I never saw or heard from that man again. It was a mystery. Maybe it was Coach Josh talking to me, or maybe it was really a man that crossed my path when I needed him.

Chapter 16

European life

I nervously waited to board the plane with an egg sandwich in one hand and my boarding pass and luggage in the other. This was going to be a long flight, longer than I'd ever been on. Sean noticed I was tense. "You okay? You're sweating a lot."

"I've never been on a long plane ride."

"You will be fine. I have done this a million times." Sean had a great personality and always looked after me. He was really a kind man.

Walking onto the plane, my anxiety escalated. I picked a seat toward the back. My luggage just above in the storage bay, I sat down in the aisle seat. It was a quick getaway in case someone stole my peanuts. The engines roared, and the plane began to slowly move and shake. I held on to the armrests with my eyes closed, knowing I couldn't escape now. There was a ding, and the pilot said, "We are ready for takeoff. Please buckle your seatbelts and enjoy the flight." I was already feeling sick. The plane left the runway, and blood rushed to my head. Breathing slowly, I told myself everything was just fine. My teammates had their sweatshirt hoods over their heads with headphones in. They didn't seem nervous at all. When it was announced we could use portable electronics, I found a movie to watch. That helped me focus and forget that I was on an airplane. About an hour later, I was having a hard time sitting still. The bathroom was free, so I took the opportunity to get up and use it. I went back to my seat and started reading a book called *The Book of Basketball*. This calmed me down for another hour. Then I got up again. I went to the bathroom to throw some water on my face. "Come on, Shawn. You can do this. Only six hours and thirty minutes left." It felt like I was on a never-ending roller coaster, and I was getting a little motion sick. Sleeping was not an option. I tried, but it never happened. Instead, I put music on. Instrumental music was the perfect accompaniment to visualizing myself playing basketball in Europe. I saw future me passing the ball to my teammates, playing good defense, and hitting the deep three pointers. I raised my hands in the air, dancing with only my hips and hands.

"Excuse me, sir."

I jumped at the sound. My trance was over. It was the flight attendant offering me a snack and drink. She politely laughed at me.

With only two hours left on the flight, I started to freak out. There was so much pent-up energy in me. As I did push-ups in the aisles, Bobby laughed at me. I yelled to him, "I want it!" Yes, I was that nutty guy on the plane that couldn't sit still.

Finally, we arrived in London. We deplaned, grabbed our luggage, and met in the middle of the airport. The first thing I needed to do was purchase a TracFone. This was how I would contact my family and friends while I was overseas. I bought the phone and minutes with euros because was less expensive than an international plan for my cell phone. After making the purchase, I texted my family to let them know we were finally in England. I looked around and took it all in "I made it," I told myself.

The coaches handed out rail passes for us to keep as we traveled for the next month and half We were going to be in London for a few days. It was too early to check into the hotel, so we walked to the London Eye. The coaches said we would have to stay up until it was dark to adjust our sleep patterns. We were all exhausted and wanted to fall asleep, but we listened anyway. The coaching staff had this system down to a science because they had been doing this for the past few years.

There was a lot going on in London. We took an awesome picture of the team and coaching staff outside Big Ben. Next, we toured the parliament. I really appreciated learning about the history of the city. London felt like New York City to me because there was so much to do, and people were everywhere. Walking around the city definitely kept us awake. After we grabbed some food, we walked back to our hotel. I roomed with two other guys, and I was grateful to have a real bed.

Our first game was against a professional team called the London Sharks. There weren't many fans at this game, so it looked like a scrimmage. The coach gave out the starting lineup, and I was not in it. This felt familiar, and I was upset. Learning from my past, I didn't let my emotions get the better of me. I had to keep up a great attitude, or it would end up like my college experiences all over again. Instead, I cheered for my team and supported the guys like a true leader should. They were watching every move I made.

With only three minutes left in the first half, I still hadn't gone in. That's when the coach yelled, "Mobilio, let's go!" I ran off the bench to the score table and snapped, "Mobilio, reporting for duty!" The scorekeeper laughed. The buzzer went off, and I jumped in. I brought the ball down the court past my defender and threw a no-look pass to a larger teammate who scored. The bench jumped up with excitement. I slapped the floor and yelled, "Defense!" It was something I had seen when I was a kid, watching the University of Connecticut team play. That's what the players did to let the other team know they were here to play defense. Bringing energy to the game was my goal. As the final seconds of the half were running down, I took the ball the full length of the court, dribbled at my defender, and put the ball under his legs. I then moved around him to get the ball back for a finish at the basket. The buzzer went off as the ball swished. The place went crazy. That shot put us only five points down at halftime.

During the second half, the coach kept the starters in the game, not swapping out for those of us sitting on the bench. The score was close. The other team was very aggressive. Unfortunately, we lost by a few points. We shook their hands and walked into our locker room. Coach Sean told me that the other team was asking about me, but they said I was just a little too short. This is what I had heard my whole life. It didn't stop me before, and it wasn't going to stop me now. I was motivated to make a bigger impression at our next game.

Our team was successful during the next five matches. We held our own against the professional teams, but I wasn't getting much playing time. Of course, I became frustrated. While guys were going out to party, I was in my room working out. I started documenting my fitness routines and posting them on YouTube. My concentration was solely on improving myself and my game.

One of our opponents was the Bristol Flyers, and we played them at a university. I was on the bench, ready for Coach to call me in, ready to make a statement. The place was sold out, and I felt like this was my chance. As patient as I could be, I waited. When Coach called my name, I ran to the table to check in. I didn't even say my name. I yelled, "I'm ready!" On the first play, I swung the ball around and got it back to the top of the three-point line. I was at NBA range. I let it go—it was nothing but net. The bench jumped up. The starting point guard cheered from the sideline. I took charge and made this game my own. Every time I jumped, the place went crazy. I was yelling and cheering with my team. We were in the "Mobilio Zone." Bristol called a time-out. When I got to the huddle, my teammates and I were still bouncing with excitement. It felt like we were all supportive of each other. This was a completely new feeling for me, to be supported by all my teammates. Coming out of the time-out, Bristol scored. I brought the ball down, swung it to the high post, and got it back out quickly in order to reverse the ball to one of our power forwards. He caught the ball in stride and slammed it, hanging on the rim. I jumped so high. I was literally losing my mind with so much excitement. He slapped my hand as he headed back down ourt. The energy was all USA. With a few minutes left, we were up five points. I approached the 3BA line again, and I was feeling awesome. I had to let it fly. When it hit the net, my defender ropped his head in disappointment. Pointing to Coach Sean on the bench, I watched as he overed his face, smiling in disbelief. We were excited for this win as we headed to the locker oom. Coach Sean said, "We have to give it to Mobilio. He was on fire." My teammates cheered, nd it felt good to be the guy on top for once.

There was little time after our win to get on the plane to Ireland. It wasn't easy playing rofessional sports; we were either on a plane, train, or bus. Sometimes it was lonely. At times, I iissed my family. But after games like the one we had just played, I was feeling too great to be onely or homesick. Coach Sean asked to speak to me as we got on the plane. He wanted to gauge iy interest in playing with the Bristol Flyers while also getting my graduate degree. The words f my custodian friend came back to me, and I realized I should consider this as an option. Coach old me he had two previous players take that opportunity, and they played while getting their iaster's degree. Honestly, I preferred a contract with a team, but I took the paperwork anyway.

The Aer Lingus plane we took to Ireland was terrifying. It sounded like it was going to fall oart. There was also no leg room, and everything felt tight. In addition, the turbulence was pretty ad. I prayed with my eyes closed for the entire flight. When we landed, Coach Sean was smiling : me. He must have been used to this.

Dublin was beautiful. There was so much land with animals everywhere. I tried to take it all ı because it felt like an awesome experience. We were entered in a tournament. So far, our xperience had been that most of the gyms were empty. In this arena, there were over two ousand fans. The announcers introduced all the players, not just the starters for the night. As ey called my name, I ran out to the middle of the court. The spotlight followed me. It was like I was in the NBA because the overhead lights were off, and the arena was lit up with fireworks and dancers. Such a different experience than our games in England.

Our starting point guard was having a great game. He was a shooting guard from Milwaukee. When I got in, my shots were knocked down, and I had a few turnovers. The coach rightly pulled me. This was really my teammate's game. I couldn't be mad at him—I had to be happy for him like he was for me our last game. Our team won the championship. It doesn't matter if you play poorly or if you don't get much playing time; it's a team win. As a team, we won, and I was happy we were holding the trophy.

There were fans outside of our locker room, and I was signing autographs. They looked at and treated us like we were NBA players. I signed as many requests as I could until Coach yelled at me to get in the locker room. I promised myself I would never forget that feeling I had as I greeted our fans. Once, I was that young boy asking for players to sign autographs for me. That night, we walked out of the gym as champions. We took our trophy out on the town that night. I had it most of the night, and I made sure the world saw that the USA won.

With our tour completed, it was time to travel home. I hadn't landed a professional contract, but that didn't mean my dream was over. There was the offer to attend university, play for the team, and get my master's degree. Some of the coaches spoke to me privately and told me that if I came back next year, they could find a place for me to play. I was willing to work and come back. Some guys took a few years to make it; others jumped right to the NBA. The coaches named me captain, which showed that they liked me. I was a leader on and off the court. I kind of forgot about the offer to play at university because playing professionally was really my dream.

Heading back home was emotional. Joe was coming to pick me up at JFK Airport. I said goodbye to my teammates and coaches. My eyes told them how I upset I was that this was all over. My brother pulled up, and I got into his car. It was silent with no music or sound. I didn't speak.

"It's okay, man," Joe quietly said.

I was upset that I didn't get picked up, so I told my brother about going for it again next year.

He looked at me and said, "You don't stop, huh?"

"No. Not until my dream comes true."

PART 5

MORE THAN BASKETBALL

Chapter 17

Back Home

"Did you have enough of this basketball yet?" I was barely up the front porch stairs when my father opened the door. Without saying anything, I casually walked by him and went to my room. He repeated it again, "Had enough, Shawn? Your dreams are over now. Get a real job." Lying in my bed, I held back my tears because I knew it was a matter of time before he came up to my room to tell me he was right.

It was my father's house, and there were only his rules. At dinner, we sat around the table with his girlfriend. He told me he knew of a job opening, and they wanted me. Great pay with benefits.

"No," I said.

He yelled, "You will go for the interview."

I began to tell him I wouldn't, and he stomped around the house telling me I was going for that interview, or I would have to leave. The timing for this confrontation was horrible. I was already emotional because I didn't receive a contract. My plan was to take a few days to process everything, to take a needed a break. Clearly, my father wasn't going allow that to happen.

The immediate thing I needed was to feel normalcy. Walking outside, I passed by my brothers. They looked at me with sympathy, but we all knew there was nothing they could do. It was like we were puppets, controlled by string. But I broke my string and said, "I am doing what have to do." Under the peaceful stars, I went outside to shoot. My father stared down at me from the top window. I kept shooting through the tears. The pain was once again my motivation.

Sleeping in my own bed felt great that night. Until 6:00 a.m. "You need to get out!" The one morning I was actually able to sleep in, and this happened.

"Why?"

"I want you out of my house, or I will have a cop escort you off the property."

"Are you serious?"

The door slammed just as he said, "Yes."

Clearly, I had no choice in this situation. I grabbed my things and packed my bag. My mother was still in Naugatuck, so I called her to explain the situation. She decided to let me stay with her for a month. On the drive there, I thought of a plan to work in a corporate gym as a fitness professional, training people toward their physical and mental goals. I had done it before, and I could do it again.

Things were going well with my mother. She was working at a local hospital. I would wake up at 4 a.m., drive her to work, and then I went to work. As the early bird trainer, I had the opening shift with morning clients. After work, I was highly motivated to keep myself physically and mentally fit for next year's basketball tryouts. The odds were against me, but this was my time to make it. I was fighting every day.

It was snowing one morning, and I barely made it to work. My boss scolded me for being late, unsympathetic to the weather conditions. A man with a T-shirt wrapped around his head ran by me as I walked through the gym. I hadn't seen him before and was curious who he was. He came around for the fifth time, so I stopped him. "Hi, I'm Shawn. What's your name?"

He mumbled some unintelligible words, then yelled with a crazy look on his face. He continued running by me. What a strange guy!

A few days went by, and I saw this man again. The way he was waving his hands, it was like he just won a gold medal. I walked over to him again and asked, "Sir, can I speak to you?"

He looked right into my eyes. I matched his gaze. He said, "You are a fighter."

"How do you know that?"

"Well, when a fighter looks into another fighter's eyes, they both make eye contact without flinching, without fear."

I smiled at him. "You're right. Did you fight?"

"A long time ago, kid. My head's all messed up now."

I needed to get back to my training, but I wanted to know more about this guy. I asked one of the managers at the front desk, "Do you know that guy who runs around?"

"Just some crazy old man," was the response.

That wasn't enough for me. There was something about him. Every morning, I engaged him ı conversation. I learned his name was Bob. The more I spoke to this man, the more I realized he /as educated and very disciplined. I suggested we start boxing together.

"I don't have the funds to do that."

"You don't need to pay the gym or me. I want to help you get back to where you were."

On my break, I would do pad work with Bob. We also worked on getting his memory back. ₁t first, it was difficult for him because he was recovering from a concussion. Bob lived in a ₃ugh neighborhood where people tended to do violent things. When I asked him what happened, ₑ laughed and told me he got jumped by five guys. This wasn't funny to me, so he told me he ₐve them his best shot. We both giggled at that statement. During our training sessions, Bob ₅ked me about my life, so I shared what I had been going through. He shared that he was a ₃ecial forces veteran. It was like God brought us together—we both needed each other to stay ₃rong. We became brothers.

I wasn't making much money from my job at the gym. I didn't have many bills, but it was ₙancially difficult for me. At one point, I had to turn off my cell phone because I just couldn't ford it. I told Dan my phone was getting shut off, and he told me I needed to keep it on. I just dn't have the cash to do it. He bought me a card to put minutes on a prepaid phone. I paid him ₁ck when I received my check. He understood that I was using the job to stay in shape, get ₓperience with clients, and have a gym when I needed it to play basketball. He also understood at a cell phone was access to opportunity. It was imperative that mine worked.

After a few months of living with my mother, our situation changed. She was going to live with her mother, my Vovó, and there wasn't room for me there. I didn't see this coming, I had no plan, and somehow, I had to find a way to make it on my own. These life punches were really knocking me down.

My car was parked outside the corporate gym, and I closed my eyes. God had kept my family and me safe. Everyone was okay. But what about tomorrow? I prayed that we would be taken care of. With no home or money, I slept in my car. The gym opened at 5:00 a.m., which allowed me time to shower before my first client. This was mentally draining, but I had a job to do. Happy clients who were motivated to work out was my business. At the end of my shift, I explained what happened to my new friend, Bob. He asked me what was going to happen next. "I'll sleep right here at the gym until I start my own gym," I told him. He smiled as he told me I would make a great general in the military.

This wasn't the first time I needed to find a place to crash. It felt comfortable figuring out how to make this situation work. Each night when the gym closed, I hid in the exercise room in the back until I saw the place was completely empty. The lights stayed on all night, but the music shut off at 10:00. During my first overnight, the music abruptly turned on at 4:00 a.m. I didn't realize it was set to a timer. I jumped, thinking someone had caught me. The automatic music timer became my alarm clock for about a month while I was staying there. To create darkness, I used a shirt to cover my eyes so I could sleep. Laundry was done in the sink, and my dryer was the sauna. It was working pretty well. I figured because I wasn't paid much, I might as well have free room and board. Most nights, I jumped into the pool because it was peaceful at night. That simple act helped me stay mentally strong. I knew I was going to make it.

My family kept in contact with me, but they never knew how I was living or surviving. I didn't want anyone worrying about me. Eventually, I found a small storefront for rent in Milford t was just enough space to start my own business. This two hundred square foot place couldn't ompare to the twenty thousand square feet the cooperate gym had, but two clients from the gym ecided to follow me. Even though many of my clients told me they would go wherever I went, adly, most of them didn't. This was frustrating at times, but it also showed me I had to work arder. The new space also gave me a new place to live. There was a small bathroom in the back where I could take care of my hygiene needs and laundry. This was truly my place.

Marketing was now part of my work, so I went out and marketed myself. Social media was a reat platform for my promotional strategy, and it was free. I also left flyers on car windshields. I alked to anyone I could to encourage them to join my new gym.

Dan continued to be supportive and always positive because he believed in me. He let me orrow an old piece of gym equipment, an all-in-one fitness machine, and he even helped me love it. Though not big, it did it all. I already had a heavy punching bag and dumbbells. It was me to make things work with what I had. Some potential clients took one look at my space and by equipment and left. Others decided to take a chance with me. It was important for me to stay a great shape so the clients would continue to believe in me. Unfortunately, my landlady had ogs, so dog hair was all over the floor. I vacuumed and cleaned every morning, but some of the air just stayed in the carpet. Some days, I had to give money back to my clients because they would have dog hair all over them at the end of their workout. This was bad for business, and it ushed me to start looking for a different place.

Bob told me the city bus wouldn't drop him off at my new location, but it would drop him off the mall. I agreed to pick him up from the mall for his training sessions with me and then drive im back to the mall. One afternoon, Bob and I went to a store that designed lettered T-shirts. We ok off the shirts we were wearing and gave them to the staff. They printed "Mobilio's Fitness" a the shirts, and we wore them around the mall as if I had a thousand clients.

"You did it," he said to me.

"We did it, buddy."

I learned that business is a team game, just like playing sports or being in the military. You can't do things on your own. My team was comprised of good friends and a lot of angels looking after me.

Driving through Milford one day, I spotted a "for rent" sign on a storefront in a great location. A lady was cleaning out the unit. She jumped when I approached, and she explained that she had just closed her business. When I explained that I wanted to rent the space, she gave me the contact information for the landlord. The owner seemed nice over the phone, and he agreed to meet with me the next day. That night, I was passing a small gym in town and saw a lot of equipment outside. It was ironic that this gym was closing, and the equipment was for sale. Immediately, I thought of the possibilities. I would have a new space in a great location with more equipment for my clients. This would be great for business! The price was very reasonable and I jumped on it.

My team came together to help me. One of my cousins brought a truck over to haul everything away. A friend let me keep the equipment in his garage for a few days. I felt like this was going to work out. I couldn't sleep because I was too busy thinking about financing and planning where the equipment would go in the new unit. It was like designing basketball game play.

The next morning, I was running on no sleep. Adrenaline would get me by through the day. I had two clients to train before I went to meet with the landlord. He was a tall Italian man who owned a lot of properties. As he showed me around, I pretended like this was my first time seeing the unit. We negotiated for a few minutes until we agreed on a deal. After shaking his hand, I walked, then skipped, to my car. This was going to look and feel like a real gym!

Chapter 18

Mobilio's Fitness

Sean from the USA Select Team called to remind me that tryouts were coming up. He wanted to make sure I would be there and ready. Even though I had been working out and training, I told him I would let him know what I was doing by the end of the week. He sounded confused, and I didn't say anything to clarify. Now was the time I would have to choose whether to try the European tour again or put all of my efforts into my business. Someone had told me most new businesses only last about two or three years. It would be a struggle. Getting a contract to play professional basketball would also be a struggle. Most people who knew me wondered how I could just give up on basketball. My whole life, I had been chasing the game, and now the game was chasing me.

I went for a walk to clear my mind and to put things into perspective. Sean would be waiting for my answer. My heart was racing. What should I choose? What if I make the wrong move? Knowing that this was my life and my sole decision, I reflected on everything that had ever happened to me. By the end of my walk, I knew what I needed to do.

I called Sean and told him I was starting my own business. He was shocked and asked me if was sure. His proposal for me to come back was that he thought a few teams might be interested. Sean didn't understand that "might be interested" was not good enough for me anymore. I declined his offer and thanked him for everything he had done. I had a new dream, and it was something I had to pursue. After we hung up, my heart told me I had made the right decision.

The new landlord accepted my payment for the first and last month's rent. Dan and I moved all my stuff into my new place. Without Dan's help, this would have been very difficult. I was o f money, so now I needed to grow my clientele. My new space was all set up. I walked around ny gym, and I used positive thoughts to keep my mind sharp. "You are going to build this usiness. You will grow. You will never give up. You will succeed. You will make no excuses." 'hese were my new mantras to keep my head in the business game. I created new motivational ards and posted them in my private space in the back, just like I had done before. Because I vould be living in my gym, I made sure I could read these statements every day when I woke up nd before I fell asleep.

I called Bob and shared the good news. He was excited to see my new place. The next day ,hen he walked in, he screamed, "YES!" Apparently, Bob was happier than I was! With only vo clients, I had to buckle down with my marketing strategy. I thought about the advice my ncle and aunt gave me when I created the non-profit to raise money for my tour of the United ζingdom. Maybe some of their advice would transfer to this situation.

There was a pizza place next door to my gym, and they were kind enough to let me put my yers on the boxes when they went out to customers. I loved the irony of pizza delivery mixed ith personal fitness. Even more, I loved getting my name out there. Next, I went from business) business to self-promote. I offered great deals for future clients. In addition, my current clients ld their friends about me, and my business grew to five. It was a slow build for my first few ionths. I offered personal training, group training, and boxing. It felt great to share my xperience as a trained boxer with my clients. It's an excellent form of exercise to punch a heavy ag, and it felt like a connection to my past.

As with most new businesses, it was hard to focus on one thing and succeed. I would have to iversify and do multiple things. By pure chance, I wandered into a recreational basketball game ie day in town. Watching the game made me realize how much I missed playing. But it also minded me of Coach Josh. Maybe I needed to coach. Through coaching, I could help younger athletes achieve their dreams, just as Coach Josh had done for me. I wasn't impressed with the coaching I saw during this game. My coaching style would help those kids play even better. The next day, I went up to the recreation department and asked how I could coach a team. I was told to grab a form from the wall and fill it out.

"You do know this is volunteer job, right?" the man behind the counter asked.

"Yes, I'm aware."

Some of my friends thought I was absolutely crazy to volunteer my time when I should be out hustling to make more money. I knew if I was going to make a name for myself in town, I might as well have fun at the same time. As we all know, winning is fun. Over the next five months, my business quickly grew, and people were starting to know my name.

Family is very important to me, and I made sure to stay connected with them. Both Joe and Mike were off living on their own. Joe had started his own business, and Mike was working in a hospital. None of us were playing basketball anymore, but we were still a team of supportive brothers. My mom continued to unconditionally support my dream, even though it had changed. My dad and I were slowly working to repair our relationship. He was happy that I was starting a business and using my talents to make money.

One day while Bob and I were training, a gentleman with hospital attire walked toward my gym door and admired our workout. Most of my clients liked privacy with one-on-one training, and I liked to respect that, so I was about to motion for this gentleman to move along. Bob indicated that he knew the man, that he was a doctor from the VA Hospital. We introduced ourselves and shook hands. Jeff agreed to sit off to the side because we were in the middle of training. After, he asked if we could talk. It felt great to say, "Come into my office." Jeff must have been impressed with what he saw because he asked if I'd be willing to train him. Bob had poken highly of me and my training abilities. I loved how word of mouth was such a great romotional tool!

For Jeff's first workout, we did a lot of boxing cardio workouts. I was wearing a warm-up hirt from the team I sponsored and coached. He asked about the team, and I told him I was oaching a rec team in town. I shared that I had convinced my brother, Mike, to coach with me, ven though he had never coached before. Bob was also a coach. Joe would come and help out hen he could. Jeff asked if he could purchase a shirt. I learned that he was from New York and ved basketball. He coached in the city for his own kid's teams.

Jeff became more interested in our team and attended games. I admired his drive to become a hysician and to maintain a hobby like basketball. Jeff was a veteran, having served in the air rce. Jeff eventually joined our coaching staff. The three Mobilio brothers, Bob, and Jeff. This as a true family endeavor. I think as a recreation team, the league had never seen that many oaches on the bench. It was all because we shared the same passion.

During the first few practices, I ran the fifth grade boys up and down the court and went over ill work. We only had one day a week for practice, and games were every Friday night. It asn't easy, and I don't think the parents or the players were expecting this much work as a creation team. But I was determined to coach like I work, through hard work. The boys picked the skills quickly. Everyone played at this age because I felt they all needed to get experience. ost of the time, I had to remind myself to go a bit easier because they were not professional ayers—they were kids. They will make mistakes, and that's okay. I had to learn how to better communicate with them. Some kids were harder to coach because they had a lot of talent, but they were lazy.

We ended the season with a winning record because the boys played their hearts out. I was proud of them. Now that my name was out there, I could create new opportunities for these kids beyond what the recreation department could offer. I developed basketball clinics for the off-season. The clinics were held at an outdoor court and were very affordable for parents. I designed them to help boys and girls develop their fundamentals. In addition, I offered one-on-one basketball training, as well as group training. Now Mobilio's wasn't just fitness training—it was also basketball training. My personal fitness business grew from seven clients to eighteen clients in three months.

To keep myself in shape, I woke up even earlier to train and stay in top basketball form and fitness. It was important for me to be able to demonstrate exercises and skills for my clients so they had a visual role model. And when you work out with them, it makes them believe in you that much more. My business grew from a service delivery model to an individualized care and commitment model. It was about showing my passion to the world. I had a real moment of clarity when I realized that God had sent me here to help others achieve their personal goals.

Now that I had diversified into two branches of services, it was time to expand again. I had most of my nights free, so I had an idea to start a group boot camp class. The first session was an introductory six week special. Ten people joined. The class was a full-body class with cardio, body weight training, weights, and strength training. What I liked about it was everyone was there to work. They each had a goal, and I made sure they were working hard to achieve their goal. A couple of boot camp clients decided they wanted more specialized training, so they became my personal clients. My rates were affordable, which made it easier for people to want to have a trainer.

None of my clients knew I was sleeping in my gym. They didn't need to know. I made sure I was catering to my clients before myself. This is how much I loved what I was doing. Attitude was important in my program. Positive energy was even more important. What you put in is what you will get out. If my clients came in tired, sleepy, or aggravated, I was there to cheer them right up. I didn't know the pain they were in, but what made my pain go away was motivating them to succeed. When they did succeed, that brought happiness to my life. All my clients were amazing and after working out with me, they understood that it was important to be mentally strong to succeed in anything they did. Working out keeps your mind strong.

Mobilio Fitness now offered personal training, basketball training, and boot camp classes. Once again, an idea came to me to add more diversity to my business. My mom's side of the family had a party, and there was a lot of dancing. While dancing, I could really feel my core muscles working hard. Everyone was having so much fun without realizing the workout they were getting. If I could earn a dance certification, I could teach dancing and add fitness moves in with it. I searched online for dancing programs, and I came across a certification that I liked. It was a three-day class. While I was getting my license, a ballroom location opened next door to my gym. I talked to the owner of the studio and asked him if he would be interested in renting out some of the space. He asked how many people I had. When I told him I didn't have any yet, he laughed. We worked out an arrangement where I would train him and his family, and he would teach me ballroom dancing. It worked out well. I got my license, and I started to promote my dance class.

One person signed up for the first class, and that was Bob. I hoped some walk-ins would attend, but no one showed up. It was just Bob and me. I still did my routine like there were twenty people in the class. Bob enjoyed every minute. That night, it bothered me that only one person showed up. I needed to promote it harder that week. Some of my clients were interested after I told them how much Bob loved it. The second class was on a Saturday at 8:00 a.m. I trained two clients before the beginning of class, and my excitement was building. Just before opening the door, I swept the floor to make sure there was no dust on it. The lights were turned on, the door was open, and I waited patiently. I had made loyalty punch cards to incentivize people to come back. After the fifth punch, the sixth class would be a free class. Finally, a car pulled up. Four women got out and walked in. I greeted them, took their class fee, and watched them step onto the dance floor. Another car pulled up, and three more people came in. One more car pulled up, and it was members of my family. They all jumped out, and we had a packed house. My mom and aunts were excited to dance. I was excited to have a successful second class.

My business was getting to a place where I was comfortable. The best part was that it was a one-man operation. I was proud of my accomplishments. Then I received an interesting phone call while I was training Jeff. A man asked me if I wanted to take over an eighth grade boys basketball program. It would be a big obligation that paid very little. I told the gentleman I would get back to him. Jeff was curious about the phone call, so we discussed it. With the growth in my business, taking on a team that practiced twice a week and had weekend games might be an issue. The time commitment could take away from my business. Jeff said, "I think you should do it. You will keep growing this way."

Chapter 19

Coaching the Youth

A potential opportunity was offered to me, and I needed to think about what I should do about it. To help me decide, I attended a tryout session for the team. The man who asked me to take over was there. It appeared like he was trying to poach players from other teams. These were kids, not the NBA! There was one player on the other team who really stood out. He'd make a great point guard for a team, especially if I was coaching. After the tryout, I was talking to the man who had called me, and I wasn't happy with the conversation. It felt like he was being shady with me. This was not going to work out for me to coach this team.

Instead, I called the coach of the other team. I explained what had happened, what I had witnessed, and also how impressed I was with their point guard. He was a parent coach and was excited when I offered to coach his team. We both recognized the mutual opportunity this could create, including the chance for these boys to play at the high school level. After our discussion, he sent out a letter to the parents introducing me with my credentials and let them know I would be coaching the team. I was grateful to be so welcomed into his basketball family.

Now that I had this new opportunity that would pay, I told the recreation league that I would not be returning. I was grateful for the opportunity to coach one season there because it showed me that I had the heart and the skills to coach. It was time to do something bigger with this newly found love.

The first day of the basketball training camp was held at an outdoor court, beginning at 7:00 am. The boys were all lined up to shake my hand, and I told them my name was Coach Mobilio. "You will not need a ball for the first two weeks," I told them. They all looked at each other incredulously. Inside my head, I was laughing. I used to think you only needed a ball to play too. After getting them all on the baseline, we ran for an hour. I told them our goal was to be in the best shape out of all the teams we would play this season. My first mission was to break the boys down and then build them back up to create a championship team. Our end game was to win it all.

I received emails from parents saying they did not want us to play against the Bridgeport league because historically the team had not done well against that league. Being from Bridgeport and playing there, I knew it was one of the best leagues and toughest in Connecticut. It was a new year, with a new coach, and we would be fine. They were not happy, but they agreed to let us try

After the two weeks of training camp, we learned plays and defenses. It took some time, but the boys were learning college offenses and defenses in eighth grade! They soaked up my philosophy and coaching. Our hard work paid off because we were winning. And I was enjoying using my game IQ to teach and strategize. We participated in league play and tournaments. The star point guard, Dylan, led the way along with two other boys, Ben and Brian. Not only did they thrive from my coaching but more importantly, they believed in themselves.

Our first season ended in a record of 38-17, with one league championship, one tournament championship, and three runner-up placements. Making it to the championship in the Bridgeport league shocked the parents as well as the boys. After that, Milford and the surrounding towns started talking about my coaching style and my players.

Trying to capitalize on my team's success, I created an eighth grade summer basketball program that would travel the tristate area to compete against other eighth grade teams. The team was named after my company, Mobilio's Fitness. Three of my players, Dylan, Brian, and Ben, came with me to play for the summer. They had bright futures and really bought into what I was doing. Our team was made up of boys from all over the state. We went on to have a winning record of 11-9 and won one championship that year that was sponsored by Under Armour. All my boys played with heart. Out of the eleven eighth grade players I coached, all of them made their high school team. Some of the boys went on to play junior varsity, and Dylan started on the varsity team as a freshman. My job was done.

Coaching came easy to me. Dealing with the parents did not. I had seen some coaches quit because of the dilemma and strain of dealing with parents. Throughout my life, I was used to adversity. I learned to handle criticism and complaints. It was easy for me to rise above and not let the parent problems bother me. My job was to help kids become the best basketball players they could be, and more importantly, the best people they could be. I truly believed in my business and my basketball program. When a coach believes, it makes clients and players believe in themselves as well. It wasn't all about winning—it was about getting those boys ready for the next level. That's what Mobilio's Fitness was about.

A friend, who was an athletic director at a local school, called to gauge my interest in running basketball camp for one week. I had a few hours open in the afternoons, so I decided to take this opportunity. These were young, energetic kids who needed to learn a little discipline. When they charged into the gym, I blew my whistle to indicate they should sit down. I would then give instructions to follow so they could learn some drills. Our first skill drill was to learn layups. They had to set up at a cone and use the proper footwork and handling to put the ball in the basket. There were about four boys who were doing this drill almost perfectly. Amazingly, three of the boys were triplets with the same birthday as me! One of the boys definitely had the heart of a champion. After the camp week was over, I asked the parents about where the kids were currently playing. They were in a noncompetitive league. This was my shot to grab these soon-to-be sixth graders and start my own feeder program into the eighth grade team. I put together my own team and learned how to schedule the games and order uniforms. I hired a graphic designer to create a website and all the logos. My original dream was growing, expanding, and becoming a reality. It occurred to me that I was subconsciously walking in the footsteps of Coach Josh. A role model then, now, and always. He must have been smiling down at me. I made sure to smile up at him every time my teams won.

After tryouts, I had thirteen boys on the roster for my new sixth grade team. Some of the boys needed more work than others, but I kept them because I knew every kid could get better. One obstacle I faced was that not every kid in a travel program will play in every game. The players who put their time in and actually worked hard on their game deserved to be on the court. I knew this from my own experience. If each player worked harder, someone would notice their hard work.

My sixth grade team started with training camp. They experienced the no ball and all running drills for the first two weeks. I figured if I could train these sixth graders right, they would be monster eighth grade players. They all worked very hard, and I even had some younger boys excel, which was awesome. It reminded me of myself when I played for Team Image. This team, and the three top players, were fearless every game. I signed them up to participate in the Bridgeport league. Unfortunately, we didn't win a single game. After the Bridgeport league, we only lost four games and made it to the championship. We didn't win the top spot that year, but the boys played amazingly. Our record for the season was 25-14. We earned four runner-up positions that year. Because of our success, I was able to recruit some new players for the fall.

For my summer basketball program, my previous players were now finishing their first year of high school. I went to a few surrounding high schools to recruit some new boys by attending freshmen basketball games. At one such game, I saw five players that I liked. I introduced myself nd my program to the coach. He was kind enough to have the five players that I liked come out

f the locker room and speak with me. I also spoke with their parents. Coincidentally, one of the

athers had already heard about me and was great at selling my program to the other parents. All

ve players joined my team. I eventually took my team to the tristate circuit sponsored by

didas. The previous year, we entered as a level B, Division II team. This year, I entered us as a

evel A, Division I team. This meant the games were going to be a lot more competitive. It was

e best way to make them better players. My coaching staff (Joe, Mike, Bob, and Jeff) and I

ere excited and having fun.

During our first tournament, we full-court pressed the team and controlled the game the

hole way. Mobilio's Fitness basketball program was growing in notoriety. We finished the

urnament 2-1. Some tournaments have so many teams playing that once you lose, you don't get

chance to play for the championship. My team had a lot of talent, but I still needed to break

eir bad habits. Many of these boys were taught to play as if it was just a run and gun game, like

ickup basketball. I knew that college coaches would be looking to see if players had game IQ

d could run an offense. Anyone could play street ball, but could they do both? We finished our

ason with a winning record of 17-9. This was one of the most talented teams I had ever

ached. There were eight players that could have started. They learned how to put their talent to

e, which made them unstoppable. It also made Mobilio Fitness unstoppable.

Chapter 20

Raise your Standards

As a young boy, I always said to myself, "One day, I will play college basketball and then play in the NBA." It's important to have high standards and lofty goals. It's also important to accept that dreams can morph and change into a whole new path. I decided not to go back to Europe and pursue a professional career there. But maybe I could still capture that dream in a different way. For instance, I might train an NBA player, or I could possibly coach a college team one day. Everyone has a personal, unique story, and there is only one Shawn Mobilio. If I can start a business and a basketball program from scratch, why couldn't I coach or train the best in the world? My work ethic, drive, and professionalism would match up to any other professional trainer or coach. Either way, I would continue to be successful. My next step was to network and do the right things to put me in the right place for those opportunities to knock at my door.

After an early morning training session with a client, I overheard some of my players talking about attending a basketball camp in town. I headed over to watch and meet the man who was running the program. He seemed like a nice guy, even if he was trying to size me up. It was obvious he had passion for the game. His name was Joe Meade, and we chatted for a little bit. We even exchanged contact information and kept in touch. Joe brought his son in from time to time to work one-on-one with me. It wasn't long before we became friends. He had a lot of knowledge because he had coached high school and college basketball and was now scouting for the Utah Jazz. He brought me to a few college games so I could see how he scouted. I admired his dedication to his job, the game, and his family. He was always on the road for the organization and that meant sometimes leaving his family. I started to help him out with his camps. Coach Joe encouraged me to go back for my master's degree in sports management. There was a program at outhern Connecticut State University that he knew about because his friend started it. He gave 1e the information, but I held off for a few months.

About this time, my friend, Robin, called me. She was a teacher and athletic director at the >cal Catholic school. Her school had an opening for a part-time physical education teacher. She ncouraged me to consider this job because she thought I would be a good fit. I had to really think bout this. Teaching at a school was not something I had considered. On the one hand, it would 1ake it difficult to train my clients, coach my teams, and continue to personally train. I would lso have a boss, and I was really getting used to being my own boss. On the other hand, I was :ill living in my gym, had no health insurance, and my income fluctuated from month to month. he idea of steady, guaranteed income was really appealing. This was the time to be quiet, pray to iod, and listen for guidance.

I went to the interview and got the job. Receiving this news told me I had followed the right ath. The new job altered my schedule a bit, as I expected. I trained clients from 4:30 a.m. until :30 a.m., then I taught from 8:00 a.m. until 2:00 p.m., three days a week. Teaching at a Catholic lementary school was a new and exciting adventure. I loved teaching children that physical ctivities can be fun. I brought discipline, structure, and even dance to gym class. The challenge >r me was the preschool children because their attention span was short. It took me a while to nd strategies to have short activities, one after the other. They started to respond positively, and e were able to have successful classes for both them and me. Parents were complimentary and njoying how their children really loved gym now that I was teaching it. I was thrilled and felt oud of myself. Teaching physical education in a school was a great way to incorporate my love of training with students. Another great thing for me was being in the Catholic atmosphere. Growing up Catholic and understanding the traditions helped me fit right in at this school.

At night, I ran my boys' basketball program and on weekends, I had games and clients. There was little time to sleep because I needed all the time to be successful at what I was doing. I loved my jobs, and I loved working hard. Most of my friends and family would ask, "How can you do all those jobs?" and tell me, "You are going to burn out." I told everyone the my candle was going to stay lit. I figured I would take on as many jobs as I could handle. If I had to give up one, I would always have my business. It actually gave me more energy taking on more jobs and challenges. Something big was going to happen to me because I had been working too hard for it not to.

Everything was looking up, until I saw my landlord one morning. He told me that he needed to raise the rent. I had been renting from him without a contract, so I asked for a contract that I would sign. That would the fair way to raise the rent. He didn't agree and threatened to kick me out if I didn't pay the rent increase. A contract would protect me, so I was unhappy that my landlord was willing to compromise.

Coach Joe was a good friend to me during this time. We were in my office looking at a sheriff's notice saying I needed to be out in thirty days. He provided a shoulder and demonstrated great listening skills, which was what I needed at that time. Here was another angel, brought to me by God, and I was thankful. I knew I would rise to the challenge of finding a new place. It wasn't an option for me to stay without a written rental agreement, especially if the landlord was going to just come in and arbitrarily raise the rent.

After two long days of searching, I came across a storefront that looked much cleaner and had heavier traffic. The rent was reasonable, and this landlord said I could move in right away. Dan and our friend Paul helped me move in when I had time between clients. The new place was a

ttle bigger but had four partition walls up that I needed to take down to make an open area for
aining and equipment. After removing the walls, I painted. The big truck tires I used for training
vere too big to fit in my car, so I literally rolled them down the street, about a mile, to the new
ocation. Most businesses close for a few weeks in order to move locations. I couldn't afford to
o that. I was motivated to get my new gym open for business as soon as possible. This
notivation included waking up at 2:30 a.m. to work a little on renovations, then train clients.
Vhen I saw my old landlord, I would just smile at him. Once he tried to talk to me. I told him to
peak to my lawyer if he had any questions.

In just seven days, my new place was all set and ready for business. My clients and friends
vere all surprised. I hadn't slept much for seven days straight, but I slept great that night. I
acrificed everything for my clients and for my business.

One of my clients suggested I go back to school for my master's degree. Jeff had mentioned
as well. And there had been an offer back on the European tour. Now there were three
uggestions that I should continue my education. Thinking I should at least check out the program
: Southern Connecticut, I met with Dr. McGinniss. He was a true gentleman and as we began to
lk, I loved his positive attitude. Throughout our conversation, I discovered that he was a well-
spected athletic director and college coach for many years. I signed up for two summer classes
at would lead me toward my master's in sports and entertainment management with a
ecialization in athletics administration. Before I left his office, he told me I needed to maintain
3.0 GPA to stay in the program. I replied, "That's it?" He smiled as I walked out. Classes would
difficult and a lot of work between my full-time jobs. But if it was easy, everyone would do it.

Coach Joe suggested we enter a summer tournament called the Nutmeg State Games in Connecticut. After doing some research, we entered the ninth grade division. A few of my players were able to stay on the team for the summer, but others had vacation or other obligations. This was a big tournament, so I needed to recruit some really tough boys to round out my team. Some of the boys I recruited had future potential to play at the college level, and one was already getting offers. I gathered them all for practice and a meet and greet.

We dominated the tournament from the start. Our talent and work ethic were too much for the other teams in our bracket. We went 4-0 that weekend, winning the gold medal and championship of the ninth grade division. Surprisingly, our success was documented in the newspapers, and we even made the news. "Mobilio's Fitness basketball program wins gold medal in the Nutmeg State games" was the headline on TV with our picture. The boys were excited. They shared it all over social media. My program was noticed, and coaches on the other teams took my information to keep in touch to set up scrimmages and games.

I had been at the Catholic school for a year when Robin, my friend and current athletic director, asked if I wanted to take over her job. Since my graduate degree would be in this area, I thought this would only enhance my opportunities, so I took it. This also put me in the financial position to get my first apartment! No more sleeping in the gym!

Another opportunity that came my way was a nice surprise. One of my professors at SCSU was on the board of directors for the National Association of Collegiate Directors of Athletics. He invited me to attend the yearly conference for this organization. What a great experience to interact and network with professionals in the field.

As of 2019, I am still in the master's program at Southern Connecticut State University. My GPA is well above a 3.0, and I am highly motivated to work hard to finish. I will graduate in May 2020. My business continues to go well. Jeff and I started to think outside the box for expansion. One of the many businesses that he owns is a massage therapy business called Norwood MediSpa, LLC. He also assists a WNBA team and professional men's lacrosse team. He continues to push me to work harder. After much discussion, we decided a collaboration was in order. We will be opening a business together called Hardwork Holdings, LLC. Finding the right space, with the right environmental conditions, to build our two businesses, Mobilio's Fitness and Norwood MediSpa, has been a challenge. However, we are not afraid of hard work, hence the name of our LLC. I finally found someone that matches my work ethic. He has taught me a lot about business and land, more than what books and classrooms can teach. I have hands-on experience and real-world expertise. As we keep searching, no one knows where this will lead to, or what town I will end up in. I do know wherever we end up, it will be the biggest and best gym/spa you will ever come across. The best feeling in life is working hard and taking the advantage of the opportunities that come your way.

Will I coach at the professional level?

Will I train professional athletes?

Or will I run twenty basketball teams out of my new location?

The future is unlimited and unmapped. All I know is that I can't stay small. I need to follow my 7 foot heart.

Nuggets of Wisdom from 7 ft Heart

I believe that if you didn't dream something, you won't achieve it.

You need practice to win, and you need to believe you will win.

In order to prevail, you need to be strong enough, and you need to believe you will succeed.

"Sometimes life doesn't go your way, but you should all stand tall and remember this lesson. Work harder and always remember to believe in yourselves." – Coach Josh

I believe that you attract what you think. So, think good things!

If opportunity doesn't knock, you need to build a door and bust through.

Winners don't make excuses—they play through it.

If you work hard and do things correctly, your time will come.

When you get to a certain level and you are comfortable, you become complacent. Never settle! Work harder and achieve the next level of greatness.

Sometimes in life you need to work differently to follow your dreams.

Build a circle around you by knowing who the right people are to support you and keep them close.

You can have all the talent in the world but if you don't work hard, you're wasting that talent, and someone else is going to take that spot.

Sometimes, you need failure to succeed.

Life is about how you handle any situation that comes at you.

If you really want something in life, you have to get it.

With no pain, there is no gain.

In life, you are going to go through hard times and that's okay.

Courage is not about medals, awards, or prizes. It's really about what you feel is right in your heart.

If you attract positive, you will receive positive.

If you really want something, you have to make it happen.

You need to make your weaknesses your strengths.

Life is short, and you need to enjoy it no matter what is thrown at you.

To be successful, you have to perfect your craft.

Basketball doesn't just teach you about the game—it teaches you about life.

Life is a team game—you can't do things on your own.

What you put in is what you will get out.

In life, it's important to have high standards and lofty goals.

The best feeling in life is working hard and taking advantage of the opportunities that come your way.

Always show them your heart.

ACKNOWLEDGEMENTS

I wish to express my sincere gratitude to Josh Ruccio, Team Image coach and Naugatuck High School boys' basketball coach. He instilled in me a passion and work ethic that I use every day in my life.

I sincerely thank Jeff and Cindy for reading my book and offering your wisdom and feedback. Heather Doughty, thank you for the editing. You did an amazing job!

I also want to thank my grandmother, God, my family and especially Joe and Mike Mobilio, Coach Bob, Coach Jeff, Coach Joe, my Mobilio's Fitness basketball teams, Antonio and Annette, Dan Bolton, my clients, and everyone who supported my journey.

ABOUT THE AUTHOR

Shawn Mobilio played college basketball at Western Connecticut State University. He was the senior captain, leading the Colonials in assists, and was ranked third in the Little East Conference. He went on to play semiprofessional basketball in London, Ireland, Scotland, and Whales.

Shawn is the owner of Mobilio's Fitness in Milford, Connecticut. As a certified athletic trainer, he works with individuals and athletes of all ages. He also manages a travel basketball program for middle school and high school players. His latest successes include coaching teams to win the 2017 Under Amour Champions 14U A Division and 2018 Nutmeg Champions 15U A Division. He is currently the athletic director and physical education teacher at St. Mary's School and is finishing his master's degree in sports management at Southern Connecticut State University.

7 ft Heart is Shawn's first book.

Made in the USA
Lexington, KY
12 November 2019